AF015

MASSIMILIANO AFIERO

AXIS FORCES 15

The Axis Forces 015 - First edition August 2020 by Luca Cristini Editor for the brand Soldiershop
Cover & Art Design by soldiershop factory.   ISBN code: 978-88-93276566   ebook 9788893276573
Copyright © 2020 Luca Cristini Editore (BG) ITALY.   No part of this publication may be reproduced, stored in a retrieval system or transmitted by any form or by any means, electronic, recording or otherwise without the prior permission in writing from the publishers. The publisher remains to disposition of the possible having right for all the doubtful sources images or not identifies.
Visit www.soldiershop.com to read more about all our books and to buy them.

The Axis Forces number 15 – August 2020

Direction and editing
Via San Giorgio, 11 – 80021 AFRAGOLA (NA) -ITALY
Managing and Chief Editor: Massimiliano Afiero
Email: maxafiero@libero.it - **Website**: www.maxafiero.it

Contributors

Tomasz Borowski, Grégory Bouysse, Stefano Canavassi, Carlos Caballero Jurado, Rene Chavez, Gary Costello, Paolo Crippa, Carlo Cucut, Antonio Guerra, John B. Köser, Lars Larsen, Christophe Leguérandais, Eduardo M. Gil Martínez, Michael D. Miller, Peter Mooney, Péter Mujzer, Ken Niewiarowicz, Erik Norling, Raphael Riccio, Marc Rikmenspoel, Samcevich Andrei, Charles Trang, Cesare Veronesi, Sergio Volpe

Editorial

Hi guys. Here is finally the new issue of our magazine, still in the midst of the global pandemic crisis. Let's hope it all ends soon and things get back to normal. This virus has already claimed many victims and caused incalculable economic damage. With our historical research and our articles, we hope to be able to alleviate all this pain and be able to resume our usual habits, to devote ourselves to our passions and above all to return to life. Our work has always continued, despite everything, and we hope that the articles contained in this new issue of the magazine will be to your liking. Of course, we always invite you to request topics and themes that all of you would like to have more covered in the magazine, in order to satisfy almost everyone. While waiting for your comments and your requests, let's now analyze the contents of this new issue: let's start with the second part of the article dedicated to the employment of the SS Totenkopf division on the Western Front, in June 1940. Following is the biography of Matthias Kleinheisterkamp, always rigorous and accompanied by many photos. We continue with the third part of the article dedicated to the employment of the Cossacks in the German armed forces. Another biography follows, dedicated to an ace of the armored units, Hans Siegel, officer first in the Leibstandarte *and then in the* Hitlerjugend. *Let's go back to the history of* Wiking *on the Eastern front in January 1943 and finally close with an interesting article dedicated to the* Panzerschreck, *the deadly German anti-tank weapon. Happy reading to all and see you next issue.*

Massimiliano Afiero

The publication of The Axis Forces deals exclusively with subjects of a historical military nature and is not intended to promote any type of political ideology either present or past, as it also does not seek to exalt any type of political regime of the past century or any form of racism.

Contents

The Totenkopf-Division on the Western Front, May-June 1940	Pag. 5
General der Waffen-SS Matthias Kleinheisterkamp	Pag. 16
Hitler's Cossacks, part 3	Pag. 39
Hans Siegel, Knight's Cross Holder of the 12. SS-Panzer Division	Pag. 52
SS-Panzergrenadier-Division Wiking on the Manytsch Front	Pag. 59
The Panzerschreck	Pag. 75

The Axis Forces

in World War Two 1939-1945

The Totenkopf-Division on the Western Front, May-June 1940
by Massimiliano Afiero

A group of *Totenkopf* soldiers after an encounter.

Totenkopf soldiers ready to spring to the attack.

On May 30, Theodor Eicke received new orders from the OKH: the *Totenkopf* had been detached from XVI.*Armee-Korps* and assigned to a quieter sector of the front, in the area of Boulogne, with coast defense duties. The SS troops were to defend the coast between Gravelines and Etaples, with strongpoints at Calais and Boulogne, against any enemy landings. This period of rest along the Channel coast allowed the division's cadre to be reorganized. Eicke received these orders in Himmler's presence, during a conference at Bailleul; the *Reichsführer-SS* wanted to personally assess the status and the behavior of the SS troops. Himmler was especially worried about the high loss of men and equipment: in ten days, during the early part of the campaign on the Western Front, the *Totenkopf* had lost 1,140 men in combat, including killed, wounded and missing. The loss of three hundred officers was the most serious problem. To fill out the division's cadre Himmler was forced to transfer to the division two hundred officer cadets from the *SS-Junkerschule* at Bad Tölz who had not yet completed their course: "...*They will be forged directly on the battlefield*", thundered Himmler. During the fighting, a large quantity of arms and equipment were also lost: about fifty trucks, numerous motorcycles, twelve anti-tank guns, eight half-tracks and an unspecified number of mortars, machine guns and rifles. Many vehicles had been damaged.

Totenkopf troops on the move towards southern France, June 1940.

Totenkopf soldiers in a French city, 1940.

At Boulogne, the maintenance personnel had to work many days to make the division's units *"mobile"* again. During the May 30 conference at Bailleul, Himmler told Eicke that he had designated *SS-Brigdf.* Kurt Knoblauch, a lackey of the *Reichsführer-SS*, as his new Chief of Staff, selected not by chance to *"check on"* Eicke. That same day, the commander of the *Totenkopf* was awarded the Iron Cross First Class for the leadership of his division during the course of *Fall Gelb*. On June 3, 1940, *SS-Staf.* Matthias Kleinheisterkamp assumed command of *SS-Tot.Inf.Rgt.3*.

Fall Rot: Plan Red, the conquest of France

On June 5, 1940, while the Battle of Dunkirk was coming to a close, the *Totenkopf* was relieved by *254.Inf.Div.* to be transferred to the Fruges-Hesdin-Frévent-Houdain sector. The second phase of the campaign, *Fall Rot*, to invade France once the Weygand Line had been overrun, had begun that morning.

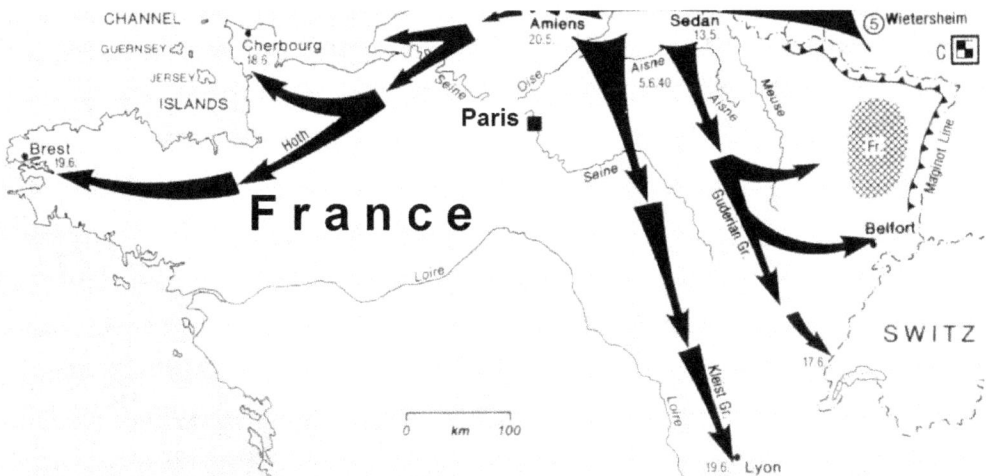

German attack axes during Operation *Fall Rot*.

***Totenkopf* signals personnel, France 1940.**

On June 7, the army detached *Hauptmann* Dingler to the *Totenkopf* staff, officially to coordinate the division's movements with those of other units of the army. After four days of fighting, the forces of *Heeresgruppe "B"* broke through the Weygand Line on the Somme and Oise. On the right wing, *4.Armee* broke deeply into French territory, while *XV.Armee-Korps* drew closer to the Seine. Further to the east, between Amiens and Péronne, *6.Armee* advanced meeting hardly any resistance. The front was also broken through on both sides of Soissons. And finally, *9.Armee* had crossed the Aisne-Oise Canal and threatened to reach the Marne. On June 9, *Heeresgruppe "A"* launched its offensive between the Aisne-Oise Canal and the Meuse. The German armies attacked across a 350-kilometer wide front, from the Channel to the Argonne. The *Totenkopf*, which was still resting south of Saint Omer, was ordered to reach the Equancourt, Moislains, Epehy, Gouzeaucourt and Trescault sector, following the Saint Pol-Arras-Bapaume road, where it would be subordinated to *6.Armee*. Meanwhile, the Germans had crossed the Seine. On June 11, the division was still in *Heeresgruppe "B"* reserve. On June 13, *Totenkopf* received orders to put itself at the disposition of *Gruppe "Kleist"*, consisting of *XIV.Armee-Korps* and *XVI.Armee-Korps*. This armored group was engaged to the right of *9.Armee* and across the Marne.

A *Czech ZB vz 53* machine gun manned by *Totenkopf* soldiers, France 1940.

A half-track of the *Totenkopf* artillery regiment.

In front of them, the French forces withdrew towards Sézanne and Romilly. Von Kleist's objective was to cross the Seine in the Troyes area. The following day, while German troops entered Paris, the division reached the *XIV.Armee-Korps* operational sector. Eicke's men spent two days seeking out enemy supply depots, freeing the roads of refugee columns and occasionally clashing with isolated enemy troops who were loath to surrender. On June 5, the Marne was crossed around 0900. The advance continued through Montmirail, Nogent-sur-Seine and Villeneuve l'Archeveque, behind the *9.Panzer-Division* columns. The *Totenkopf* covered 340 kilometers in thirty-six hours.

Nogent-sur-Seine area: *Totenkopf* soldiers speaking with tankers of *9.Panzer-Division*. In the photo is a *PzKpfw.IV* of *Panzer-Regiment 33*, France 1940.

SS-Staf. Kleinheisterkamp (center) with Theodor Eicke.

On June 16, the division was ordered to follow the *10.Pz.Div.* that was at Clamecy. *SS-Tot.Inf.Rgt.1* had to attack Joigny and *SS-Tot.Inf.Rgt.3*, Laroche. On June 17, in order to surround the French troops still deployed along the Maginot Line, *Panzergruppe "Guderian"* attacked from the Langres plateau towards Besançon. The objective of *Panzergruppe "Kleist"* was to cut off the retreat of French troops between Dijon and the Swiss border. *XVI-Armee-Korps* was thus sent to the Dole-Dijon sector. The

XVI.Armee-Korps crossed the Loire at Nevers and continued its advance towards the Saône. The *Totenkopf* continued its march by following the *10.Pz.Div.* towards Lyons. At 1340, on the road to Lormes, a French plane strafed a column of *4.Kp./SS-Tot.Inf.Rgt.3*, causing one dead and four wounded. A truck was destroyed.

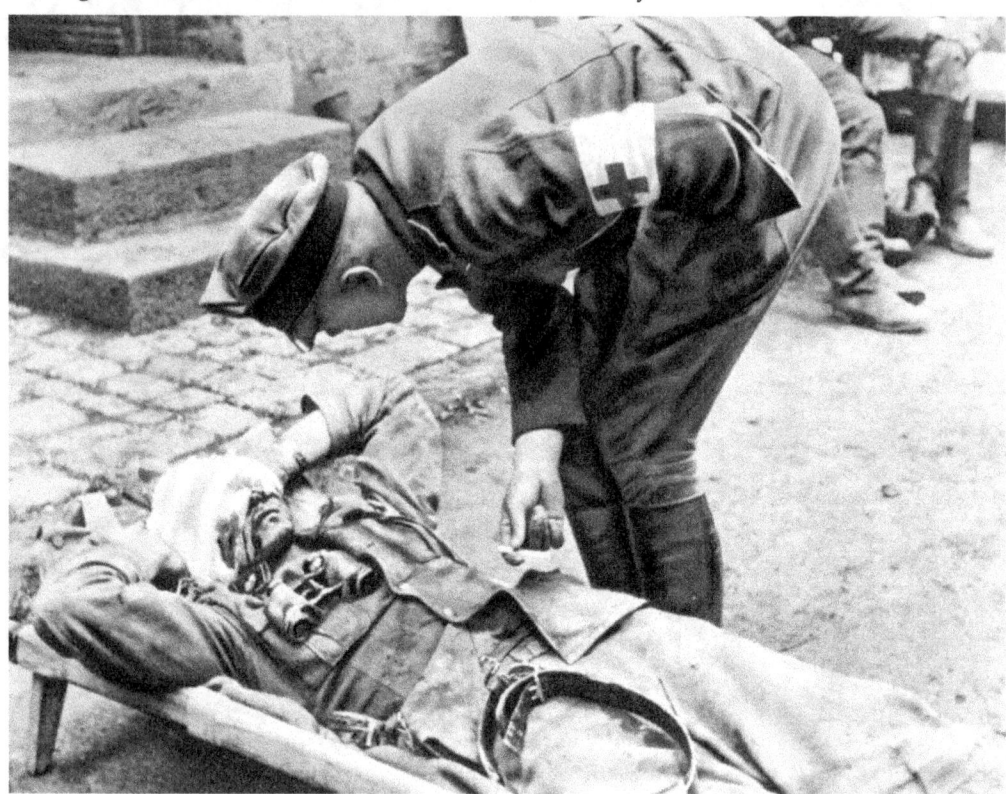

A *Totenkopf* officer with a serious head wound, France 1940.

Totenkopf soldiers attacking a French village, 1940.

The aircraft was shot down. On the left flank of the corps, the *SS-Verfügungsdivision* had to face French attempts to break through to the south from Chatillon-sur-Saône. To avoid any threat, *SS-Tot.Inf.Rgt.2* was placed in reserve in the Coulanges-sur-Yonne area.

On June 18, while the French government requested armistice terms from the Germans, the *Totenkopf* reached Chateau-Chinon and Montceau-les-Mines. From there, the SS division continued its advance, in accordance with orders imparted by Hitler: "...*Pursuit of defeated troops must be maintained with the utmost energy*".

Totenkopf soldiers marching in a French village, June 1940.

Totenkopf motorcyclists, 1940.

SS-Tot.Aufkl.-Abteilung in action

On June 19, the division's reconnaissance group seized a bridge over the Loire at Digoin. In the meantime, Lyons had been declared an "open city" and the Germans intended to use its intact bridges over the Rhône and the Saône. On the French side, the Army of the Alps was to attempt to protect its northern wing and its rear area, directly threatened by the German advance towards Lyons and the Rhône-Alpes region, while at the same time fighting against Italian troops. Therefore, General de Mesmay established a defensive line between Tarare and the Saône, with orders to block National Routes 6 and 7. For this task, he had the 25th Tirailleurs Sénégalais Regiment, supported by other troops. Around 1630, the *SS-Tot.Aufkl.-Abteilung* of *SS-Stubaf*. Hierthes, coming from Thizy and d'Amplepuis, broke into Tarare; some French soldiers were disarmed near the cemetery without any fighting. The SS scouts then continued along the road towards Paris, but at Zehr they ran into a barricade defended by a handful of French soldiers from the 131st Infantry Regiment. The encounter was brief but sharp: the SS lost five men, among them *SS-Hstuf*. Kemmetmüller, the recon unit's adjutant, and five wounded.

Totenkopf motorcycle scouts engaged in an attack against a French village, supported by a captured *Panhard* armored car, June 1940.

A *Totenkopf* officer observes the attack, 1940.

The French soldiers were finally dislodged by fire from 37 mm *Pak 36* guns and took refuge in the woods, but they were all captured the next day. The SS scouts continued their advance along *RN 7* and took the village of Pontcharra, which was also defended by enemy troops who had been cut off. The advance continued towards Arbresle. The area was defended by the 2nd Battalion of the 25th Tirailleurs Sénégalais Regiment, which had left the city at dawn in order to avoid victims among the civilian population.

Totenkopf soldiers with French prisoners, 1940.

Totenkopf motorcyclists on a French road, 1940.

A *Totenkopf* truck on the move, June 1940.

The Senegalese riflemen had taken up positions on the Cornu, a hill that dominated Arbresle and its approaches, the valleys of the Brévenne and of the Turdine. A barricade of tree trunks had been erected halfway along the road on the hill towards the cemetery. The SS scouts were taken under fire by the Senegalese near the Brévenne bridge. *II./SS-Tot.Inf.Rgt.1* then arrived as reinforcement, in particular the *5.Kp./1* under *SS-Hstuf.* Ernst Häussler. Other elements of the division were staled near the bridge over the Turdine. The *5.Bttr./SS-Totenkopf-Art.-Regiment* under *SS-Hstuf.* Kausch arrived to support the attack and began to hit the Senegalese positions. The houses in which they had taken shelter were destroyed one after another. Around 2130, the SS troops prepared to mount an attack against the Cornu, after having lengthened their artillery fire. The *5.Kp.* and the *6.Kp./SS-Tot.Inf.Rgt.1* crossed the bridge over the Brévenne and continued on towards Eveux. Shortly after, the Senegalese riflemen began to fall back towards Yseron. Nevertheless, some of the troops continued to hold out, especially in the Collomb and Vially houses and in the Vially farmhouse at Rompières. In the end, they were surrounded by Totenkopf soldiers. During the clashes that ensued, fighting was hand-to-hand and with hand grenades in the two houses, while the farmhouse was set ablaze.

A *Totenkopf* motorcyclist dispatch rider, France 1940.

On the morning of June 20, *II./SS-Tot.Inf.Rgt.1* continued its southward advance towards Sourcieux and Sant-Bel. Further to the east, the *1.Kp./SS-Tot.Inf.Rgt.1* under *SS-Hstuf.* Kurtz also advanced. The SS troops moved ahead at great speed, as Theodor Eicke had ordered. Kurtz's men were however again stalled before the village of Lentilly, where the remnants of the 2nd Battalion of the 25th RTS had entrenched themselves, suffering heavy losses. Shortly after, elements of *4.(s)Kp.* and of *13.(IG)Kp./SS-Tot.Inf.Rgt.1* arrived to reinforce Kurtz's men. The *5.Kp./SS-Tot.Inf.Rgt.1* tried to attack Lentilly from the flank, but was also stopped cold by accurate fire from the Senegalese. The Germans then called upon their artillery that emplaced its batteries in the village of Mollières.

A *Panhard* armored car captured and used by *SS-Totenkopf-Aufklärungs-Abteilung*, 1940.

A *Fieseler Storch* flew over the area and provided precise coordinates to the artillerymen, who opened fire to great effect. The French colonial troops in turn suffered heavy losses and the SS troops took advantage to break into the village and pounce on the enemy; after some close-quarter fighting, the Senegalese were forced to surrender.

Totenkopf **soldiers who have been awarderd the Iron Cross, during the French campaign, 1940.**

After crossing the Marne, the *Totenkopf* announced that it had captured 6,088 prisoners. On June 21, the *Totenkopf* entered Villefranche-sur-Saône, where it seized a large quantity of arms and at Saint-Sorbin, where it captured more than 1,300 French soldiers. At the end of the day the division was ordered to cease its offensive to the south and to turn to the north in order to join up with *XIV.Armee-Korps* at Orléans. The following day the Franco-German armistice was signed at Rethondes. On June 23, the division arrived at Bonny-sur-Loire on the Loire with orders to regroup in the area of Noyant-Méon-Saint Paterne-Château du Loir. *Gruppe "Kleist"*, minus the *XVI.Armee-Korps*, had been ordered to reach the line Royan-Saintes-Angoulême-La Rochefoucauld. It then was to cross all of France from east to west to then reach the Atlantic coast, from the Gironde to the Pyrenees. The *Totenkopf* troops and those of the *SS-Verfügungsdivision* were to occupy the Côte d'Argent (Silver Coast) south of Bordeaux as far as the Spanish border. The "cease fire" was to begin on June 25. The French campaign had cost the division 339 killed, of whom were 18 officers, 881 wounded, of whom 34 were officers, and 32 missing. These losses were quite high when considering the number of effective combat days. Nonetheless, the performance of the *Totenkopf* troops could be considered satisfactory.

Bibliography
M. Afiero, "*Totenkopf*", Marvia Edizioni
M. Afiero, "*3.SS-Pz.Div. Totenkopf - Vol. I: 1939-1943*", Associazione Culturale Ritterkreuz
M. Afiero, "*The 3rd Waffen-SS Pz.Div. Totenkopf 1939-1943: Vol.1*", Schiffer Publishing
M. Afiero, "*Totenkopf I: 1939-1942*", Almena Ediciones

General der Waffen-SS Matthias Kleinheisterkamp
A Biographical Chronology
by Michael D. Miller
with translation assistance from Gary Costello

A formal portrait of Matthias Kleinheisterkamp wearing the Knight's Cross of the Iron Cross and the Finnish Order of the Cross of Liberty, 1st Class with Oak Leaves and Swords in 1943 (*Roger Bender*).

A formal portrait of *SS-Sturmbannführer* Kleinheisterkamp as *Chef des Stabes* of the *Inspektion der SS-Verfügungstruppe*, 1936. (BA, SS-Personalakte Kleinheisterkamp).

SS-Sturmbannführer Kleinheisterkamp oversees training exercises at *SS-Führerschule* Braunschweig (M.Yerger).

Matthias Kleinheisterkamp
SS-Obergruppenführer und General der Waffen-SS

Born: 22.06.1893 in Elberfeld/Bergisches Land.

Suicide(?): 02.05.1945 near Halbe/Kreis Feltow in Soviet captivity, after capture by Soviet troops in the "Kessel von Halbe" on the night of 29./30.04.1945. His vehicle was found by German troops, abandoned, with his driver dead inside, and Kleinheisterkamp was declared missing in action (per Andreas Schulz and Dr. Dieter Zinke, *Die Generale der Waffen-SS und der Polizei, Band 2*, p. 511). Veit Scherzer, in *Die Ritterkreuzträger 1939-1945*, indicates only "*v.[ermisst] 29.04.1945 bei Halbe.*" E.G. Krätschmer gives "*Vermißt seit 2. Mai 1945 bei Halbe.*" Jost Schneider states "*Suicide: 8.5.1945 near Halbe, Germany, Eastern Front.*" Mark C. Yerger, in *Waffen-SS Commanders, Augsberger to Kreutz*, writes: "*... while leading a rear guard action in Fortress Halbe, Kleinheisterkamp was captured during combat the night of April 29/30, 1945, and committed suicide as a prisoner the following week.*", with the added footnote: "Sources vary as to the actual date of his death, either May 2nd (also given as date he was listed as missing) or May 8th." The *Volksbund Deutsche Kriegsgräberfürsorge e.V.* lists him as missing since 08.05.1945.

NSDAP-Nr.: 4.158.838 (Joined 01.05.1937)
SS-Nr.: 132.399 (Joined 01.11.1933)

Promotions
02.08.1914: *Fahnenjunker* (*mit Wirkung vom 01.08.1914*)
31.10.1915: *Leutnant* (*ohne Patent*; 00.00.1918: Granted *Patent vom* 12.11.1914; 00.00.1922: Granted *RDA vom* 01.09.1915 [7])
01.02.1928: *Oberleutnant* (26)
01.10.1929: *Hauptmann* (5)
01.11.1933: *SS-Bewerber*

SS-Stubaf. Kleinheisterkamp at *SS-Führerschule* Braunschweig (*Mark Yerger*).

08.01.1934: *SS-Anwärter*
24.01.1934: *SS-Mann*
08.02.1934: *SS-Sturmmann*
10.02.1934: *SS-Scharführer*
12.02.1934: *SS-Oberscharführer*
14.02.1934: *SS-Truppführer*
19.03.1934: *SS-Obertruppführer*
12.04.1934: *SS-Sturmführer*
17.06.1934: *SS-Obersturmführer*
20.04.1935: *SS-Hauptsturmführer*
01.06.1935: *SS-Sturmbannführer*
20.04.1937: *SS-Obersturmbannführer*
18.05.1940: *SS-Standartenführer*
19.07.1940: *SS-Oberführer*
09.11.1941: *SS-Brigadeführer und Generalmajor der Waffen-SS*
01.05.1943: *SS-Gruppenführer und Generalleutnant der Waffen-SS*
01.08.1944: *SS-Obergruppenführer und General der Waffen-SS*

Career

ca. 1897-ca. 1901: Attended *Volksschule*.

ca. 1901-00.08.1914: Attended the *Städtisches Gymnasium* (through *Quarta*) and the *Städtisches Realgymnasium* in Elberfeld (graduated *Oberprima* and passed his *Abitur*).

02.08.1914-00.10.1914: Entered service as *Fahnenjunker*, assigned to *1. Westfälisches Pionier-Bataillon Nr. 7* (Köln-Riehl).

00.10.1914-00.10.1914: Briefly assigned to *1. Lothringische Infanterie-Regiment Nr. 130*.

00.10.1914-00.01.1919: Assigned to *Reserve-Infanterie-Regiment Nr. 219*, successively posted as a *Zugführer*, *Bataillons-Adjutant*, *Regiments-Adjutant*, and *Kompanie-Offizier*. Deployed to the Western Front: 00.00.1914-00.00.1915; Eastern Front: 00.00.1915-00.00.1916; Western Front again: 00.00.1916-00.00.1918. Severely wounded on one occasion (shrapnel in the head).

00.01.1919-00.03.1919: Assigned to *Infanterie-Regiment 605* and as *Leiter* of the *Demobilisierungskommando* (demobilization headquarters) of *Reserve-Infanterie-Regiment 55* (in *VII. Armee-Korps*).

Kleinheisterkamp addresses SS officer cadets at Braunschweig in 1935 (*Mark Yerger*).

SS-Stubaf. Kleinheisterkamp discusses tactical training with fellow officers at Braunschweig (*Mark Yerger*).

01.02.1919-00.10.1919: *Adjutant* of *Freikorps "Lichtschlag"* in the area of Hagen (in the Ruhr area). Established on 14.12.1918 by order of *Generalleutnant* Oskar von Watter commanding *VII. Korps* in Münster), it was commanded by *Hauptmann* Otto Lichtschlag and numbered some 2530 men. The unit was known for considerable brutality, and after several instances of murderous violence against striking workers in Dorsten and Bottrop became known as *"Freikorps Totschlag"* (manslaughter)

00.10.1919-31.12.1920: Assigned to *III. Bataillon/Schützen-Regiment 7* in the *Freikorps Freiwilliges Garde-Landesschützen-Korps von Neufville"*.

01.01.1921-31.03.1929: Transferred to the *Reichswehr*, assigned successively as a *Zugführer* in *I. Bataillon/ Infanterie-Regiment 17* (Braunschweig), and as *MG-Offizier* and *Mob-Offizier* of *II. Bataillon/Infanterie-Regiment 17* (Göttingen).

01.04.1929-30.09.1933: *Chef* of *5. Kompanie/Infanterie-Regiment 17*, then of *15. Kp./Infanterie-Regiment 6* (Ratzeburg).

01.10.1933-01.02.1934: *"Hauptmann beim Stabe"* and *Regimentsadjutant* of *Infanterie-Regiment 6* (Lübeck).

01.11.1933: Joined the *Allgemeine-SS*.

08.01.1934-07.03.1934: *Referent Ia* (*Ausbildung* [training]) with *SS-Abschnitt XIII* (Stettin).

01.02.1934: Discharged from the *Reichswehr* at his own request.

07.03.1934-12.04.1934: *Referent Ia* to *SS-Oberabschnitt Nord* (Hamburg-Altona).

12.04.1934-15.06.1934: *Referent für Ausbildungswesen* to the staff of *SS-Oberabschnitt Nord*.

15.06.1934-01.04.1935: *Ausbildungs- und Sportreferent* to *SS-Oberabschnitt Nord*.

00.08.1934-31.03.1935: Assigned as *Beauftragter für Ausbildung* to the staff of the *Politischen Bereitschaft Hamburg* (the later *SS-Standarte "Germania"*).

01.04.1935-01.04.1936: Entered the *SS-Verfügungstruppe*, assigned as a *Taktiklehrer* (tactics instructor) to the *SS-Führerschule Braunschweig*. In a recommendation for Kleinheisterkamp's promotion to *SS-Sturmbannführer*, dated 29.05.1935, the commander of the school, Paul Hausser, wrote:

SS-Hauptsturmführer Kleinheisterkamp was a war participant [i.e., Veteran of World War I/MdM], is a very good tactician with great experience, combined with the ability to give very clear instruction; very eager and conscientious, good comrade.
Very suitable for promotion.
The Führer of SS-Führerschule Braunschweig m.d.F.b.
[signed] Hausser- SS-Standartenführer
(SS-Personalakte Kleinheisterkamp)

01.04.1936-01.06.1938: *Chef des Stabes* of the *Inspektion der SS-Verfügungstruppe* (under Paul Hausser).

01.05.1937: Joined the *NSDAP*.

00.10.1937: Subject of legal proceedings by an *SS* court based on the following charges, as listed in a letter of 22.09.1937 from the *Chef SS-Hauptamt* (August Heissmeyer) to the *Inspektion der SS-Verfügungstruppe*:

- Incurring debts and failing to meet economic obligations.
- Starting a long business trip without providing his family with the necessary funds to cover living expenses...
- Rumors of a relationship with another woman

(*SS-Personalakte Kleinheisterkamp*)

16.05.1938: Letter from the *Chef der SS-Personalkanzelei*, Walter Schmitt:

To Obersturmbannführer Kleinheisterkamp.
With regard to the Inspection der ᛋᛋ-Verfügungstruppe. The Reichsführer SS has ordered that:
1. You are suspended from duty with immediate effect.

Reason:
On the 7.5.1938, you made a derogatory remark with regard to the Leibstandarte-SS "Adolf Hitler" in the presence of a Major of the Reichsheer and leading members of the Schutzstaffel. Furthermore, in a later conversation with ᛋᛋ-Hauptsturmführer Schuldt, you made belittling comments against ᛋᛋ-Obergruppenführer Dietrich. This matter will be handed over to the ᛋᛋ-Gericht for further investigation.
2. Should there be further use for you in the Schutzstaffel after the SS court has completed its investigation, it will under no circumstances be in the Verfügungstruppe but rather you will be required to carry out your duty in the Allgemeine ᛋᛋ.

Der Chef der Personalkanzlei.
(*SS-Personalakte Kleinheisterkamp*)

21.06.1938: Formally punished with a *"strenger Verweis"* (strict reprimand) *"wegen mangelnder Eignung"* (due to lack of aptitude), specifically his disparaging remarks against the *Leibstandarte-SS "Adolf Hitler"* and toward its commander, *SS-Obergruppenführer* Josef (Sepp) Dietrich. The reprimand read as follows:

On 7.5.1938, in the presence of several leaders of the Schutzstaffel and a Major of the Wehrmacht, you made a derogatory statement about the Leibstandarte-ᛋᛋ "Adolf Hitler". For your tactless and ᛋᛋ-damaging [*ᛋᛋ-schädigendes*] behavior, you deserve severe punishment. Regarding your later conversation with ᛋᛋ-Hauptsturmführer [Hinrich] Schuldt, the content of this conversation could not be determined beyond any doubt. In view of the fact that it is a statement of hearsay, the accusation against you of having verbally belittled ᛋᛋ-Obergruppenführer Dietrich through statements is dropped.
(SS-Personalakte Kleinheisterkamp)

Flugplatz Oberwiesenfeld, München, 22.09.1938. French Prime Minister Édouard Daladier arrives for discussion of the Sudeten crisis with Hitler. Right to left: Daladier, an unknown *SS-Hauptsturmführer*, Reich Foreign Minister Joachim von Ribbentrop, *SS-Obersturmbannführer* Matthias Kleinheisterkamp, and *Gauleiter* Adolf Wagner.

04.08.1938: Revocation of his dismissal from the *SS-Verfügungstruppe*.

04.08.1938-01.09.1938: Reinstated in *SS-Verfügungstruppe* and attached to the staff of *SS-Standarte "Deutschland"* (München).

01.09.1938-01.12.1938: Officially assigned to the staff of *SS-Standarte "Deutschland"*.

The Axis Forces

Flugplatz Oberwiesenfeld, München, 29.09.1938: British Prime Minister Neville Chamberlain arrives on German soil for the third and final time, in order to sign the Munich Agreement ("for the cession to Germany of the Sudeten German territory"). From right to left: Sir Neville Henderson (British Ambassador to Germany), *Reichsstatthalter* Franz Ritter von Epp, Chamberlain, *SS-Obersturmbannführer* Kleinheisterkamp, and Reich Foreign Minister Joachim von Ribbentrop.

SS-Staf. Kleinheisterkamp during Western Campaign (*Rikmenspoel*).

01.12.1938-04.06.1940: *Führer* of *III. Sturmbann/SS-Standarte "Deutschland"* (later redesignated *III. Bataillon/SS-Regiment "Deutschland"*). He led this unit in the Polish Campaign and the Netherlands. Succeeded by Carl Reichsritter von Oberkamp.

03.09.1939-00.10.1939: *Kommandeur* of *Gefechtsgruppe "Kleinheisterkamp"*, formed around his *III. Sturmbann/SS-Standarte "Deutschland"*. This was one of three combat groups comprising the mixed *Heer/SS-VT Panzer-Division "Kempf"* in the invasion of Poland (the others were *Gruppe "Steiner"* [under *SS-Standartenführer* Felix Steiner] and *Gruppe "Landgraf"* [under *Oberst* Franz Landgraf]). Among his responsibilities during the Polish Campaign was the evacuation of foreign diplomats and their families from Warsaw to Königsberg, which he accomplished using a 60-vehicle transport column;

his efforts resulted in the successful relocation of 178 diplomats and 1,200 other foreign subjects from the Polish capital.

04.06.1940-07.07.1941: *Kommandeur of SS-Totenkopf-Infanterie-Regiment 3/SS-Totenkopf-Division* in France and later Russia. Succeeded *SS-Staf.* Hans-Friedemann Goetze (killed in action at Lestrem, 27.05.1940). Command of the Regiment was briefly held (07.07.1941-18.07.1941) by *SS-Ostubaf.* Hellmuth Becker when Kleinheisterkamp took the reins of the Division after the wounding of Theodor Eicke on the 6th of the month. On 29.09.1940, Eicke assessed the Kleinheisterkamp as follows:

Evaluation of SS-Standartenführer Kleinheisterkamp, Kommandeur of SS-Totenkopf-Inf.-Rgt. 3

<u>Age:</u> 47, <u>Married:</u> yes, <u>Children:</u> 5, <u>last promotion date:</u> [No entry made; last promotion date was 01.07.1940]

<u>Character:</u> Open and direct

<u>Person:</u> A person of strong individual character who does not tolerate weak superiors. Always strives to achieve completion. Always appears to be self-assured and confident; ambitious but not in a negative way.

SS-Standartenführer **Kleinheisterkamp during the Western Campaign, his uniform devoid of collar insignia for security purposes** (*Bundesarchiv, SS-Personalakte Kleinheisterkamp*).

<u>National Socialist:</u> Advocates the Movement without reservations and recognizes it as the basis for noble soldiering.

<u>Soldier:</u> An experienced player, does not adhere to any particular formula: is tough and dogged when carrying out his decisions. Has the courage to take responsibility.

<u>Overall evaluation:</u> He can be depended upon, especially in difficult situations. It would be difficult to live without him. Misjudged, as he cannot deal with inconsistent superiors.
Kleinheisterkamp is suitable for the leadership of a larger formation.

Signed E i c k e
ᛋᛋ-Gruppenführer
Generalleutnant.
(*SS-Personalakte Kleinheisterkamp*)

June 1940: *SS-Standartenführer* Kleinheisterkamp meets with *Reichsführer-SS* Himmler and *Gruppenführer* Wolff.

June 1940: *SS-Staf.* Kleinheisterkamp, now commanding *SS-Tot.Inf.Rgt.3*, decorates NCOs and enlisted men with the Iron Cross Second Class for bravery during the Western Campaign (*NARA, SS-KB Ernst Baumann*).

Eicke's attitude toward Kleinheisterkamp appears to have changed by January 1941, when he inflicted a *"schweren Verweis"* (severe reprimand) upon him. Charles Sydnor writes:

> Himmler was... enraged by Eicke's habit of listing the punishments of officers publicly in division orders, and by his practice of disciplining high-ranking SS officers as though they were privates. The Reichsführer's anger was aroused particularly when Eicke ordered Standartenführer Kleinheisterkamp, a regimental commander, confined to quarters allegedly for failing to carry out an order, and then published the news of Kleinheisterkamp's punishment in a special circular to all units in SSTK.

(Sydnor, citing Himmler letter to Eicke, dated 30.01.1941. [Bundesarchiv Koblenz, NS-19/370], in *Soldiers of Destruction*, p. 127, fn. 12)

07.07.1941-18.07.1941: *Führer* of *SS-Division "Totenkopf"* (*"vertretungsweise beauftragt mit der Führung beauftragt"*). He was temporarily assigned as a substitute for the wounded Theodor Eicke. Succeeded by Georg Keppler and returned to his regimental command. During his brief command, and following the capture of the town of Opotschka, Kleinheisterkamp reported to Himmler on the casualties of *SS Division "Totenkopf"* recorded thus far in Operation Barbarossa. Sydnor writes:

According to the figures given Himmler, the Totenkopfdivision in sixteen days of fighting had lost 82 officers and 1,626 NCOs and enlisted men killed, wounded or missing- nearly ten percent of the division's combat strength. This serious casualty rate brought quick criticism from General [Erich von] Manstein, who felt the losses were disproportionate to the relatively modest gains made by SSTK during the first weeks of fighting.

(Kleinheisterkamp to Himmler, 09.07.1941 [Bundesarchiv Koblenz, NS/19-370], in ibid, pp. 167-168 and p. 168, fn. 26)

Kleinheisterkamp and *SS-Totenkopf-Division* commander Theodor Eicke present decorations in the aftermath of the Western Campaign (*Roger Bender*).

15.07.1941 - 27.10.1941: Returned to duty as Kommandeur of SS-Totenkopf-Infanterie-Regiment 3, reassuming command from Hellmuth Becker. Relieved of command by Divisionskommandeur Eicke and sent home to the Reich under simultaneous assignment to the Führerreserve. Becker then took permanent command of the unit with effect from 25.10.1941. Charles Sydnor writes:

On October 27, [Eicke] relieved Matthias Kleinheisterkamp of his command and sent him home for an indefinite leave. The reason given [in a letter to Karl Wolff dated 28.10.1941, in Bundesarchiv Koblenz, NS/19-370] was that Kleinheisterkamp's nerves had been shattered by the fighting on the [River] Pola and that he needed a lengthy rest. Eicke's real reason was probably personal, since he intensely disliked Kleinheisterkamp. In any event, his act violated a standing order by Himmler forbidding the transfer of any senior unit commander in the Waffen-SS without his express approval. When he learned of what had happened, Himmler sent Eicke a stiff written reprimand, accusing him of disobeying orders just to satisfy his own jealousy and spite. Eicke was warned- for the last time, Himmler said- that such actions would have severe repercussions (*SS-Personalakte Eicke*, Himmler to Eicke, November 28, 1941) (Sydnor, *Soldiers of Destruction*, p. 200, fn 76)

29.11.1941-01.01.1942: Attached to the *Kommandoamt der Waffen-SS* in the *SS-Führungshauptamt*.

Matthias Kleinheisterkamp after his 1 July 1940 promotion to *SS-Oberführer* (*Roger Bender*).

01.01.1942-01.04.1942: *Führer* (*m.d.F.b.*) of *SS-Division (mot.) "Reich"* on the Eastern Front. Succeeded Wilhelm Bittrich. Succeeded by Georg Keppler. In a *Tagesbefehl* (Order of the Day) issued 11.01.1942, the newly appointed divisional commander declared:

Men of the proud SS-Division "Reich"!
On 9 January 1942, I took command of the Division. I am aware of the honour, as an old member of the Division, to lead you over the winter months. Your deeds, your readiness, your attitude and discipline are exemplary in the history of the Waffen-SS and the Army. I am convinced that under my leadership you will continue to use all your strength to maintain and secure the success you have achieved. It is my pleasure to convey the warmest greetings and best wishes of your Division Commander, Generalleutnant Hausser, who would like to return to you as soon as possible. In grateful reverence we remember our dead and wounded comrades.

[signed] Kleinheisterkamp Generalmajor
(Otto Weidinger, *Kameraden biz zum Ende*, p. 170)

As a result of his courage and leadership during the difficult fighting in this period, he was recommended a third time for the *Ritterkreuz* by *General der Panzertruppe* Heinrich von Vietinghoff, receiving the award on 31.03.1942 (see "Decorations & Awards", below).

01.04.1942-15.12.1943: *Führer* (*m.d.F.b.*; appointed as full *Kommandeur*, 01.06.1942) of *SS-Gebirgs-Division "Nord" (mot.)*, which was then being reformed at *Truppenübungsplatz Wildflecken*. In June 1942, he led the Division to Finland. There it was united with *SS-Kampfgruppe "Nord"* under *SS-Oberführer* Han Scheider and operated against Soviet forces in Karelia as part of *20. Gebirgs-Armee* (under *Generaloberst* Eduard Dietl). It was redesignated *6. SS-Gebirgs-Division "Nord"* on 22.10.1943. He was succeeded by Lothar Debes. During his tenure as *Kommandeur* of *"Nord"*, he enjoyed a good working relationship with *Generaloberst* Dietl. The following is excerpted from Kleinheisterkamp's letter to Himmler of 22.05.1943:

... I would like to inform you that Generaloberst D i e t l was with the Division on 19 May and expressed his very special appreciation and thanks to the Division for its front-line achievements, for its attitude, work and diligence. Herr Generaloberst was proud of the Division and wanted to give recognition to it. Herr Generaloberst offered the badge of the Gebirgsjäger, the Edelweiss. I thanked him very much....The development of the Division is making good progress. It is the backbone of the XVIII.Geb.A.K., whose leadership I handed over to General Böhme again on 19.5. (*SS-Personalakte Kleinheisterkamp*)

Summer 1942: *Generaloberest* **Eduard Dietl** (*Oberbefehlshaber* of *20. Gebirgs-Armee*) in conversation with Kleinheisterkamp during an inspection of *SS-Gebirg-Division "Nord"* (NARA, *SS-Kriegsberichter* Ittner).

Dietl and Kleinheisterkamp (*Ittner*).

02.08.1942: Meeting with Himmler at Kananeinen during the *Reichsführer*'s official visit to Finland. On the same day, he and *General der Infanterie* Franz Böhme (Commanding General of *XVIII.(Gebirgs) Armee-Korps*) escorted Himmler during his inspection of *Division "Nord"*. (*Der Dienstkalender Heinrich Himmlers 1941-42*, p. 505)

25.09.1942-00.10.1942: Held acting leadership of *XVIII.(Gebirgs)Armee-Korps* during the absence of its commanding general, *General der Infanterie* Franz Böhme (per Mark C. Yerger and Ignacio Arrondo, *Totenkopf, Volume 1*, p. 175).

09.10.1942: Received the following secret letter of reprimand from *Reichsführer-SS* Himmler for excessive consumption of alcohol and harassment of subordinates. He was nearly relieved of command for this misconduct.

I received your report from 23.8.1942 and also the strange explanation from ᛋᛋ-Sturmbannführer [Eugen] Kunstmann [*Ia* of *"Nord"*], who - as I know - was also drunk and the biggest agitator. I have asked the SS judges to send me the same report that you also requested. I can only express my deepest disapproval of this entire incident. You have more than sufficiently earned your replacement as divisional commander. As a Hauptmann or a battalion commander you could, on occasion, allow yourself the odd faux pas. After I trusted you to run a Division despite my serious misgivings, you had to realize that the time for getting plastered [*besaufen*] - if you want to count this as one of the highlights of your life - is over once and for all. I only refrained from deposing you because of the impression the transfer would make on the Wehrmacht, and then I would have to say openly why I deposed you. The fact that you let all those disgusting drinking scenes, egged on by your loyal assistant [*Adlatus*] Kunstmann, take place in the presence of a major of the Wehrmacht, particularly characterizes you. The way in which you let other people drink cognac, in abuse of your superior relationship, even pouring out your glass under the table, shows me a character flaw, which you will have to work hard to eradicate before your service ends. If proof had been needed of how necessary these SS judges are, it was amply provided by you and your drunken Führerkorps that night and on that morning.

Left: *Divisionskommandeur* **Kleinheisterkamp and his men applaud a performance in 1942. Right:** *SS-Brigadeführer* **Kleinheisterkamp with Lieutenant General Siilasvuo (1892-1947), Commanding General of the Finnish III. Korps to which the "*Nord*" Division was assigned.**

Kleinheisterkamp (far right) is interviewed together with Lieutenant General Siilasvuo.

I have already transferred ᛋᛋ-Hauptsturmführer [Hans] Zentgraf since I cannot expect this man to serve under a commander who treated him so degradingly and indecently. ᛋᛋ-Sturmbannführer Kunstmann will also be transferred immediately. I will deny him the ability to work as a staff officer for two years and will give him a battalion, under an appropriately strict commander, in an infantry regiment. You yourself will be aware that this will have been the first and last case of such behavior. I expect you not to drink any more alcohol for the next two years, as at age 49 you are not yet able to handle it. You will need to settle the money matters concerning the "Black Fund" [*Schwarzen Fonds*] as quickly as possible. For the future, any money from such funds is untouchable for you. These funds are not intended to be used for private purposes.

Signed: H. Himmler (*SS-Personalakte Kleinheisterkamp*).

Kleinheisterkamp (right) walks along a snow-packed road with *Generaloberst* Dietl (*Andrey Zubkov*).

15.12.1943-01.05.1944: In *Führerreserve der Waffen-SS, SS-Führungshauptamt*.

01.01.1944-30.04.1944: *"beauftragt mit der Aufstellung"* (charged with formation) of *VII. SS-Panzer- Korps*.

25.02.1944-16.04.1944: *Vertreter des Kommandierenden Generals* (deputy to the Commanding General) of *III. (Germ.) SS-Panzer-Korps*, Felix Steiner (recovering from illness).

01.05.1944-01.07.1944: *Kommandierender General* of *VII.SS-Panzer-Korps*, comprised of *10.SS-Pz.Div. "Frundsberg"* and *17.SS-Pz.Gren.Div. "Götz von Berlichingen"*. He was the only holder of this short-lived command which was absorbed into *IV. SS-Panzer-Korps*, again under his command.

01.07.1944-20.07.1944: *Führer (m.d.F.b.)* of *IV. SS-Panzer-Korps*. Succeeded Walter Krüger. Succeeded by the *Chef des Stabes* of the *Korps*, Nikolaus Heilmann, who briefly held command until 06.08.1944 when he was succeeded by Herbert Otto Gille.

20.07.1944-01.08.1944: In *Führerreserve der Waffen-SS, SS-Führungshauptamt*.

01.08.1944-30.04.1945: *Kommandierender General* of *XI. SS-Armee-Korps* (upgraded as *XI. SS-Panzer-Korps*, 01.02.1945). He was the sole commander of this formation, established 24.07.1944 at Ottmachau bei Neisse from the remnants of *V. Armee-Korps*. Throughout its existence, it was comprised only of *Heer* units, as follows:

Generalkommando XI. SS-Armee-Korps			
Date	Subordinated Divisions	Armee	Heeresgruppe
15.08.1944	545.Gren.Div.; Gruppe Oberst Schmidt; 544.Gren.Div.; Elements of 78.Gren.Div. and 8.Pz.Div.	A.O.K. 17	Nordukraine
31.08.1944	545.Gren.Div.; 78.Gren.Div.; 544.Gren.Div.	A.O.K. 17	Nordukraine
28.09.1944	208.Inf.Div.; 545.Gren.Div.; 78.Gren.Div.	A.O.K. 17	Nordukraine
13.10.1944	96.Inf.Div.; 208.Inf.Div.; 545.Volksgren.Div.; 78.Sturm-Div.	A.O.K. 17	Süd
05.11.1944	96.Inf.Div.; 208.Inf.Div.; 545.Volksgren.Div.; 78.Sturm-Div.	A.O.K. 17	A
31.12.1944	320.Volksgr.Div.; 545.Volksgr.Div.; 78.Sturm-Div.	A.O.K. 17	A

21.01.1945	320.Volksgren.Div.; 545.Volksgren.Div.	A.O.K. 17	A
26.01.1945	5.ung.Res.; Kgr. 253.Inf.Div.; 320.Volksgren.Div.; 545.Volksgren.Div.	Armeegruppe Heinrici (1.Pz.Armee)	Süd
Generalkommando XI. SS-Panzer-Korps			
01.02.1945	Kgr. 4.Geb.Div.; 253.Inf.Div.; 320.Volksgren.Div.; 545.Volksgren.Div.	Armeegruppe Heinrici (1.Pz.Armee)	Süd
19.02.1945	Pz.Gren.Div. "Kurmark"; 25.Pz.Gren.Div.; Festung Küstrin	A.O.K. 9	Weichsel
01.03.1945	712.Inf.Div.; 25.Pz.Gren.Div.; Festung Küstrin	A.O.K. 9	Weichsel
31.03.1945	712.Inf.Div.; Pz.Gren.Div. "Kurmark"; 169.Inf.Div.	A.O.K. 9	Weichsel
12.04.1945	712.Inf.Div.; 169.Inf.Div.; 303.Inf.Div. "Döberitz"; 20.Pz.Gren.Div.; 9.Fsch.Jäg.Div.; Pz.Gren.Div. "Kurmark"	A.O.K. 9	Weichsel
30.04.1945	337.Volksgren.Div.; 169.Inf.Div.; 214.Inf.Div.; 275.Inf.Div.; 286.Inf.Div.; 342.Inf.Div.	A.O.K. 9	Weichsel

(Kurt Mehner, ed, *Die Waffen-SS und Polizei 1939-1945, Führung und Truppe*, pp. 127-129)

An informal portrait of Matthias Kleinheisterkamp, 1942 (*Andrey Zubkov*).

In an assessment dated 27.12.1944, *General der Infanterie* Friedrich Schulz, commanding *17.Armee* (under which Kleinheisterkamp's *Korps* was then assigned), wrote:

A purposeful Commanding General who leads his units with a firm hand, strong-willed, demands a lot from himself and his units. Has not yet been under my command in the big fight, therefore cannot yet be judged conclusively.

[signed] Schulz
General der Infanterie
Mit der Führung der 17. Armee beauftragt.
(*SS-Personalakte Kleinheisterkamp*)

04.02.1945-11.02.1945: *Führer* (*m.d.F.b.*) of *III.(germanische) Panzer-Korps*. Succeeded Georg Keppler. Succeeded by *Generalleutnant* Martin Unrein.

06.02.1945: In a *Beurteilungsnotizen* (evaluation notice) of that date, *Generaloberst* Heinrici (*Oberbefehlshaber* of *Armeegruppe Heinrici*) wrote: Upright, confident personality. Very energetic, active, brave. No outstanding talent, but a practical troop leader with great experience, a healthy tactical eye, who asserts his will over the troops even in

A signed portrait of Kleinheisterkamp, 1942 (*Andrey Zubkov*).

difficult situations. During the 14 days of subordination [to Armeegruppe Heinrici], he proved to be a determined and crisis-proof leader, and through natural insertion into demands, that made it difficult for him to fulfill his mission, he cooperated particularly well. (*SS-Personalakte Kleinheisterkamp*)

28.04.1945: Received orders from 9. *Armee* to break out of the Halbe Kessel at 1800 hours. At that time, Kleinheisterkamp's command post was located in the forest of Klein Hammer near Hermsdorf.

29./30.04.1945: Captured by Soviet troops in the Halbe Kessel. His vehicle, with his dead driver, was later found by German troops. Kleinheisterkamp remained missing.

Decorations & Awards

* **09.05.1945:** *Eichenlaub zum Ritterkreuz des Eisernen Kreuzes* (871.) (posthumously) as *SS-Obergruppenführer und General der Waffen-SS* and *Kommandierender General* of XI. *SS-Armee-Korps*/9. *Armee*/*Heeresgruppe Weichsel*, Eastern Front

* Per Veit Scherzer, *Die Ritterkreuzträger 1939-1945*, Kleinheisterkamp's status as an Eichenlaub recipient cannot be fully clarified on the basis of existing documentation in the *Bundesarchiv*. He writes that Walther-Peer Fellgiebel's *Die Träger des Ritterkreuzes des Eisernen Kreuzes, 1939-1945* refers to a *Fernschreiben* (telegram) from *Oberbefehlshaber 9. Armee* (*General der Infanterie* Busse), which reached the *Heerespersonalamt* on 21.04.1945, recommending the award for Kleinheisterkamp; Fellgiebel goes on to state that a note was added to the proposal: "*Dienstwegvorschlag bzgl. Sofortverleihung abwarten*" [await official proposal with regard to an immediate award]). This unofficial *Fernschreiben* does not appear in the *Bundesarchiv*, nor does the awaited official proposal. Scherzer writes that the telegram vanished and was never processed, because the liaison officer of the *Waffen-SS* to *HPA/P5a*- Wilhelm Kment- took it in hand and [attempted to?] hand it over to the *Reichsführer-SS* for endorsement. Had Himmler done so, it would have been returned to Berlin for a final decision, the approval of Hitler, and completion of an immediate award. But this did not occur. On the basis of available documents, it appears that *General* Busse informed *Heeresgrupe Weichsel* as well as the *Chef Heerespersonalamt* (*General der Infanterie* Wilhelm Burgdorf) of the award proposal; The unanswered question is whether or not Hitler made the direct award (as reported by E. G. Krätschmer; in a letter to Gerhard von Seemen of 07.08.1980, Krätschmer wrote that the case for Kleinheisterkamp's Oakleaves

was indeed decided and the award presented (together with the immediate awards for Kurt Hartrampf, Friedrich Blond, Edgar Haukelt, and Gustav Reber); he added that the awards were announced via radio message from *Führerhauptquartier*, Berlin to *General* Busse's *9. Armee* (surrounded in the Halbe Kessel) on 28.04.1945.

Kleinheisterkamp in conversation with *General der Infanterie* Franz Böhme (Commanding General of *XVIII.(Gebirgs)Armee-Korps*) in the late Summer of 1942. Visible between them in the background is *Generalmajor* August Krakau (*Führer* of *7. Gebirgs-Division*).

Kananeinen, Finland, 02.08.1942: Kleinheisterkamp and *General der Infanterie* Franz Böhme accompany Himmler during his inspection of *SS-Gebirgs-Division "Nord"*.

The incoming radio messages of 9.Armee for the month of April 1945 no longer exist, and wireless connections to the Berlin Führerbunker had been cut since 0500 hous on 28.04.1945. In Scherzer's view, the award was neither approved nor rendered, based on the following: *General* Burgdorf would not have a) handed a proposal over to the Führer without first having the opportunity to review and approve it himself (which would have been impossible as he did not have a detailed proposal on his desk and approvals by superior commands (*9. Armee, Heeresgruppe Weichsel* [*Generaloberst* Gotthard Heinrici], and Kleinheisterkamp's *SS* superior, Himmler) were not available to him; and b) *General* Burgdorf would most probably not have short-cut this decision for an immediate award without waiting for the official proposal, which was still enroute through the official channels. The award number "871" was assigned by the *Ordensgemeinschaft der Ritterkreuzträger e.V.* [*OdR*].

Kananeinen, Finland, 02.08.1942: Kleinheisterkamp and *General der Infanterie* Franz Böhme accompany Himmler during his inspection of *SS-Gebirgs-Division "Nord"*.

Matthias Kleinheisterkamp in Karelia, 1942.
(*Roger Bender*)

31.03.1942: *Ritterkreuz des Eisernes Kreuz* as *SS-Brigadeführer und Generalmajor der Waffen-SS* and *Kommandeur* of *SS-Division (mot) "Reich"/9. Armee/Heeresgruppe Mitte*, Eastern Front. *Vorschlag* submitted by *General der Panzertruppe* Heinrich von Vietinghoff, *Kommandierende General* of XXXXVI *Panzer-Korps*. In a letter of 17.03.1942, von Vietinghoff wrote:

As acting division commander of SS Div.Reich, Brig. Führer Kleinheisterkamp has once again proved himself outstandingly during the particularly difficult winter battles from January 10 to March 15; he is a leader that you can rely on in every situation and was proposed by me for the Ritterkreuz (*SS-Personalakte Kleinheisterkamp*).

Two recommendations were previously submitted, by Paul Hausser and Theodor Eicke, but disapproved by higher authority:

"*Vorschlagsliste Nr. 4 für die Verleihung des Ritterkreuzes des Eisernen Kreuzes*", submitted by *SS-Oberführer* Felix Steiner, *Kommandeur* of

SS-Brigadeführer und Generalmajor der Waffen-SS **Kleinheisterkamp in 1942.**

SS-Standarte "Deutschland" and endorsed 18.07.1940 by *SS-Gruppenführer und Generalleutnant der Waffen-SS* Paul Hausser, *Divisionskommandeur* of the *SS-V.-Division*:

After a forceful crossing of the Bevelund Canal in Zeeland on 16.05.40, which his Battalion had to fight hard for, the III. Rgt. ᛋᛋ "D" advanced with great speed - partly on bicycles - and took control of the causeway from Bevelund to Walchern. On that day, around 900 Frenchmen remained in the hands of the battalion. On the following day the battalion under the most difficult conditions and after more than 8 hours of fighting, forcibly crossed the 1.5km-long - on both sides bordered by inaccessible swamps - connecting causeway from Bevelund to Walchern, whose whole eastern front was defended in a planned and tough manner by new French forces with a strength of about 2 regiments. At 20.00 hours, the enemy resistance was crushed. Vlissingen was taken in a nighttime chase. Here, around 4000 prisoners remained in the hands of the Regiment. Thanks to the passionate energy, tenacity and bravery of Obersturmbannführer Kleinheisterkamp and his troops. the Regiment smashed a complete French division on Zeeland and took Vlissingen. Moreover, he and his Battalion did an excellent job in the western theater of war, as well as breaking through the dams on the eastern part of the island of Bevelund, which were mined by the Dutch, flooded and defended by the French. In the Polish campaign he led one of the 3 Gefechtsgruppen [battle groups] of the Panzer-Division Kempff [sic, Kempf] during a large part of the campaign. He distinguished himself through prudent, bold and energetic leadership of the mixed battlegroup he led, as well as at Mlawa and Modlin, his Battalion, the III./Rgt. ᛋᛋ "D". He was awarded the clasp to the EK1 and EK2.

[Signed] Steiner. ᛋᛋ-Oberführer and Kommandeur of ᛋᛋ-Standarte "Deutschland".

Approved!
Kleinheisterkamp is a proven, exemplary battalion commander. During the battle for the dam on the island of Walchern, he was in the forefront, I personally observed the he carried out reconnaissance, use of heavy weapons and storm troops himself or under his direction, and thus laid the foundations for success. The severity of the fighting is evident from the Regiment Commander's statement. The rapid success of the advance at Vlissingen indirectly influenced the battle for Antwerp.
 [Signed] Hausser - ᛋᛋ-Gruppenführer and Divisionskommandeur.
(*SS-Personalakte Kleinheisterkamp*)

A studio portrait of *SS-Brigadeführer und Generalmajor der Waffen-SS* **Matthias Kleinheisterkamp, wearing a fur-lined greatcoat.**

"Vorschlagsliste Nr. 4 für die Verleihung des Ritterkreuzes des Eisernen Kreuzes", signed 06.07.1941 by *SS-Gruppenführer und Generalleutnant der Waffen-SS* Theodor Eicke, *Divisionskommandeur* of the *SS-Totenkopf-Division*:

Mission as per Korpsbefehl Nr. 13 of 3.7.1941

SS-T.Div. first reaches Rosenow and southward as ordered in two columns. Mission: Protection of the flank of LVI. A.K. Through a bold plan of attack and despite a strong enemy presence, SS-Oberführer Kleinheisterkamp succeeded in taking Rosenow (Zilupo) by surprise on 4 July 1941 at 10:30 a.m. and capturing the bridges intact.

Mission of LVI. A.K. on the 6.7.1941:

"Early on 06.07.41 and in a pincer movement, the SS-T.Div. attacks the enemy on the heights east and southeast of Rosenow, defeats him and pushes forward to Sebesh. After reaching the road Sebesh-Opotschka, the division proceeds under cover to the south and southeast along the road to Opotschka." Under the tight leadership of its regimental commander, the SS-T Inf.Rgt. 3 achieved unimaginable things on this day and the following days. The breakthrough of the Stalin Line, which was made up of numerous strong concrete bunkers and in which the opponent was in possession of all dominant terrain points, was made possible by the masterly leadership of SS-Oberführer Kleinheisterkamp, who was on the front line in the ever changing situations during this difficult battle, and who was again and again, through his quick and sure decisions, the driving force of the attack. To make things more difficult, this battle had to be carried out without Flak or air support. In the night from 6th to 7th July 41, when the Division commander was seriously wounded, SS-Oberführer Kleinheisterkamp took over command of the Division on the orders of the Division commander and from this time until the arrival of the new division commander he led the division during the intense fighting, especially around Sebesh and Hill 202 as well as around Opotschka and Porchow. Following an intense counterattack by the Russians and due to a shortage of ammunition, on the night of the 8.7.41, Hill 202 was lost again and when on the same night the 290 I.D. received the order to relieve the SS-T.Div., SS-Oberführer Kleinheisterkamp made the decision to attack again, in order to be able to hand over a completed combat operation to the 290 I.D.. After the capture of the strongly defended city of Sebesh and having recaptured Hill 202 the area was handed over to the 290 I.D. Through his strong personal commitment and his calm and confident leadership even in the most difficult of battles, SS-

Oberführer Kleinheisterkamp led not only his regiment but also the division to great successes. SS-Oberführer Kleinheisterkamp, who already proved himself in the Poland and Western Campaigns, was already recommended for the award of the Ritterkreuz of the Eisernes Kreuz on 16.06.40 by the commander of the SS-V.Div.. I ask that SS-Oberführer Kleinheisterkamp, in appreciation of the decisive successes achieved by him, be awarded the Ritterkreuz of the Eisernes Kreuz. (*SS-Personalakte Kleinheisterkamp*)

Hanko, Finland, 01.06.1943: The *Kommandeur* of *SS-Gebirgs-Division "Nord"* pauses for a smoke as he speaks with a Finnish colonel (*Finnish Wartime Photograph Archive - Photo #128797*).

Hanko, Finland, 01.06.1943: *Divisionskommandeur* Kleinheisterkamp with *SS-Obersturmbannführer* Constantin Heldmann (far left) and two adjutants (*Finnish Wartime Photograph Archive - SA Kuva, Photo #128798*).

SS-Gruf. Matthias Kleinheisterkamp on 1 May 1943, at his desk in Finland (NARA, *SS-Kriegsberichter Ittner*).

02.10.1939: *1939 Spange zum 1914 Eisernes Kreuz I. Klasse*
13.09.1939: *1939 Spange zum 1914 Eisernes Kreuz II. Klasse*
00.00.191_: *1914 Eisernes Kreuz I. Klasse*
00.00.191_: *1914 Eisernes Kreuz II. Klasse*
01.09.1942: *Kriegsverdienstkreuz I. Klasse mit Schwertern*
20.04.1942: *Kriegsverdienstkreuz II. Klasse mit Schwertern*
00.00.191_: *Ritterkreuz II. Klasse mit Schwertern des königlich sächsischen Albrechtsordens*
ca. 1918: *Verwundetenabzeichen, 1918 in Schwarz*
00.00.1942: *"Winterschlacht im Osten 1941/42"*

A formal studio portrait of *SS-Gruppenführer und Generalleutnant der Waffen-SS* Kleinheisterkamp in 1943 (Roger Bender).

12.03.1944: Kleinheisterkamp, as acting Commanding General of *III.(Germ.)SS-Pz.Korps*, presents the *Ritterkreuz* to officers of *11.SS-Div. "Nordland"*.

ca. 1939: *Medaille zur Erinnerung an die Heimkehr des Memellandes*
ca. 1939: *Spange "Prager Burg" zur Medaille zur Erinnerung an den 1. Oktober 1938*
ca. 1939: *Medaille zur Erinnerung an den 1. Oktober 1938*
ca. 1938: *Medaille zur Erinnerung an den 13.03.1938*
ca. 1920: *Schlesisches Bewährungsabzeichen 1. Stufe*
ca. 1920: *Schlesisches Bewährungsabzeichen 2. Stufe*
ca. 1934: *Ehrenkreuz des Weltkrieges 1914-1918 mit Schwertern*
00.00.193_: *Deutsches Reichssportabzeichen in Bronze*
[01.12.1936]: *SA-Sportabzeichen in Bronze*
00.00.193_: *Deutsches Reiterabzeichen in Bronze*
[01.12.1936]: *Ehrendegen des Reichsführers-SS*
[01.12.1936]: *Totenkopfring der SS*
00.02.1934: *Ehrenwinkel für alte Kämpfer*
16.05.1943: <u>*Vapaudenristin 1.luokka (VR 1)*</u> (Order of the Cross of Liberty, 1st Class with Oak Leaves and Swords) (Finland)

Notes
*Son of the railway secretary Matthias Kleinheisterkamp and his wife Anna, née Rüpper.
*Religion: Protestant until 00.00.19__, then declared himself *"gottgläubig"*.
*Married on 27.03.1921 to Ellen Heusing-Esch (born 04.07.1900 in Frankfurt am Main, died 14.10.1943 after a long illness). Three sons (born 11.04.1922; 12.04.1928; and 18.09.1937) and two daughters (born 15.09.1923 and 11.12.1929) resulted from this marriage.

Kleinheisterkamp in 1943 (*M.Rikmenspoel*).

03.11.1944: *SS-Ogruf.* Kleinheisterkamp decorates *Oberfeldwebel* Walter Rappholz.

Sources

Mehner, Kurt: *Die Waffen-SS und Polizei 1939-1945, Führung und Truppe*. Militair-Verlag Klaus D. Patzwall, 1995.

Miller, Michael D. & Schulz, Andreas: *Leaders of the SS & German Police, Volume 1: Reichsführer-SS – SS-Gruppenführer (Hans Haltermann to Walter Krüger)*. R. James Bender Publishing, 2015.

National Archives and Records Administration, College Park, Maryland: *SS-Personalakte of Matthias Kleinheisterkamp*. Microfilm document collection A3343SS.

Schulz, Andreas & Zinke, Dr. Dieter: *Die Generale der Waffen-SS und der Polizei 1933-1945, Band 2 (Hachtel-Kutschera)*. Biblio-Verlag, 2005.

SS-Personalkanzlei and SS-Personalhauptamt: *Dienstaltersliste der Schutzstaffel der NSDAP, Stand vom 1. Oktober 1934*.
- *Dienstaltersliste der Schutzstaffel der NSDAP, Stand vom 1. Juli 1935*.
- *Dienstaltersliste der Schutzstaffel der NSDAP, Stand vom 1. Dezember 1936*.
- *Dienstaltersliste der Schutzstaffel der NSDAP, Stand vom 1. Dezember 1937*.
- *Dienstaltersliste der Schutzstaffel der NSDAP, Stand vom 1. Dezember 1938*.
- *Dienstaltersliste der Schutzstaffel der NSDAP, Stand vom 30. Januar 1942*.
- *Dienstaltersliste der Schutzstaffel der NSDAP, Stand vom 20. April 1942*.
- *Dienstaltersliste der Schutzstaffel der NSDAP, Stand vom 9. November 1944*.

Sydnor, Charles S.: *Soldiers of Destruction: The SS Death's Head Division, 1933-1945*. Princeton University Press, 1977.

Weidinger, Otto: *Kameraden biz zum Ende: Der Weg des SS-Panzergrenadier-Regiments 4 "DF" 1939-1945*. Plesse-Verlag, 1962.

Williams, Max: *SS Elite, Volume 2*. Fonthill Media, 2017.

Witte, Peter &Wildt, Michael, etc.: *Der Dienstkalender Heinrich Himmlers 1941-42 im Auftr. Der Forschungsstelle für Zeitgeschichte in Hamburg bearb*. Hans Christians Verlag, 1999.

Yerger, Mark C.: *Waffen-SS Commanders: Augsberger to Kreutz*. Schiffer Military History, 1997.
- *German Cross in Gold Holders of the SS and Police, Volume 1 ("Das Reich:" Kurt Amlacher to Heinz Lorenz)*. R. James Bender Publishing, 2003.
- *Totenkopf. The Structure, Development and Personalities of the 3. SS-Panzer Division, Volume 1* (with Ignacio Arrondo). Helion & Co., 2015.

Hitler's Cossacks
by Sergio Volpe – part 3

Two Cossack volunteers on top of their horses.

Cossack female veterinarian inspecting a horse.

The exodus of the Cossacks

In early 1943, following the rapid retreat of the forces of the Group of Armies A, the Cossack territories were abandoned. The capital of the Don Cossacks, Novotcherkassk, fell into the hands of the Soviets on February 5. Thousands of Cossacks from Don, Kuban and Terek fled with their women and children, under the protection of the units created by the *Ataman* Pavlov. This long march ended near Novogrudok in Belarus, a territory assigned by the Germans to the Cossacks. Another group of Cossacks was grouped under the orders of von Pannwitz in Kherson, Ukraine, employed by the General Staff of Army Group A. Immediately afterwards, Pannwitz went to the Kuban bridgehead, to give new impetus to the organization. of his units. But, once again, the evolution of the military situation thwarted the Cossack project. On January 26, 1943, Pannwitz was ordered to deal with the defense of Feodosia, on the southern coast of Crimea. Pannwitz carried out the mission with the help of two Cossack regiments from the Kuban, under the orders of the Oberst Kulakov and numerous other Cossack departments of the Don and Terek. It was only in early April, when he was allowed to leave Crimea, that Pannwitz was able to return to work on his large Cossack unit.

Formation of the 1st Cossack division

In early April 1943, the OKH decided to grant Pannwitz all his requests. The General Staff assigned the Cossacks the Mielau (Mlawa) training camp, north of Warsaw. Before the war, this camp had been used by Polish cavalry units. Mielau became the educational center of the 1st Cossack Division officially formed on April 21, 1943. In late April, the first convoys left Kherson for Mielau with soldiers, women, children and horses.

Oberst **Helmuth von Pannwitz.**

Two Cossack volunteers in a training camp, 1943.

A group of Cossack volunteers, 1943.

The existing Cossack units did the same: the Lehmann regiment, the von Wolff regiment from Poltava, the Jungschulz regiment from Kiev and the Kononov regiment from Mogilev. To complete the division's staff, recruitment campaigns were launched in the prison camps. The announcement about the formation of a large Cossack unit attracted a large number of Cossack officers who emigrated after the Russian Civil War (1917-1920) and who had moved to France, Croatia or Serbia. With the arrival of the first volunteers in Mielau, training began immediately, not without difficulty, considering the heterogeneity of the troops. The Cossacks were full of enthusiasm but were also unwilling to submit to harsh German discipline. The most difficult task for von Pannwitz, however, was not education and discipline, but rather being able to make the German cadres understand the Cossack mentality, fundamental for the success of his mission. The commander of the Cossack division first set the example, learning the Russian language and studying Cossack history and traditions. Despite being Protestant, but appreciating the spiritual and mystical richness of the Orthodox religion, commander von Pannwitz did not hesitate to participate in all the religious ceremonies organized by the Cossacks. This made him very popular among his Cossack people.

A 3rd Kuban Cossack Regiment.

A German officer with a Cossack volunteer, 1943.

A *Gefreiter* of the 2nd Siberian Cossack Regiment.

To eliminate all tensions, Pannwitz relieved the German officers who failed to adapt to the Cossack mentality, regardless of their military worth. Three colonels, von Schulz, von Knalben and Lehmann formed the backbone of the division. Important commands were assigned to German officers, all others to the Cossacks. The language continued to represent a problem but in the end this obstacle was also overcome, with the introduction of a sort of internal military language which overcame all linguistic misunderstandings.

Uniformological notes

In order for the Cossacks to be aware of the continuity of their traditions and their history, Pannwitz authorized the traditional Cossack uniform. But this uniform was worn only on solemn occasions by a squadron and the commander's bodyguard. On all other occasions, the volunteers always wore a mixture of elements of the feldgrau and Cossack uniforms. And so the volunteers continued to wear colored stripes on their trousers, already in use in the imperial army: wide red thread for the Cossacks of the Don, narrow red for those of the Kuban, blue for those of the Terek and yellow for those of Siberia. The Cossacks of Don and Siberia were also allowed to wear papakha, the high lambskin headdress with a red background for the former and yellow for the latter.

A group of Cossack officers of the 5th Don Regiment.

Generalmajor **von Pannwitz and Cossack volunteers.**

Similarly, the Cossacks of the Kuban and those of the Terek wore the Kubanka, a headdress in lambskin, with a red background for the former and blue for the latter. Finally, all the Cossacks carried on the left sleeve of the feldgrau uniform, the badges with the colors of their territory of origin. The Cossacks of the 1st Regiment of the Don wore a shield in blue and red cloth on the right sleeve, those of the 5th Regiment on the left sleeve. The Cossacks of the 3rd

Kuban Regiment wore a red and black shield on the left, while those of the 4th Regiment on the right. The Cossacks of Siberia wore a yellow and blue shield on the top of their right sleeve. Also to stimulate the patriotism of the Cossacks, Pannwitz formed a divisional band, including large drums mounted on magnificent white horses. These drums were used to open the march of horsemen or infantrymen.

A group of Kuban Cossacks on the Eastern Front, 1943.   Terek Cossack volunteer.

German Cossack officer during training, 1943.

Organization

On June 1, 1943, Pannwitz was promoted to *Generalmajor*. Three months later, in September 1943, the training of the 1st Cossack Division was completed. At that time, it was made up of two brigades, each consisting of three cavalry regiments. The First Brigade (*I. Kosaken Reiter-Brigade Don*), under the orders of the *Oberstleutnant* Frh. Hans von Wolff, included:

- 1st Cossack Regiment of the Don (*Don-Kosaken Reiter-Rgt.1*), under the orders of the *Oberstleutnant* Graf zu Dohna

- 2nd Cossack Regiment of Siberia (*Sibirische Kosaken Reiter-Rgt.2*), under the orders of the *Oberstleutnant* Freiherr von Nolcken

- 4th Cossack Regiment of the Kuban (*Kuban-Kosaken Reiter-Rgt.4*), under

The Axis Forces

Oberstleutnant **Freiherr Hans von Wolff.**

Major **Ewert von Renteln in France, 1944.**

the orders of the *Oberstleutnant* Freiherr von Wolff.

The Second Brigade (*II.Kosaken Reiter-Brigade Kosaken*) included:

- 3rd Kuban Cossack Regiment (*Kuban-Kosaken Reiter-Rgt.3*), under the orders of the *Oberstleutnant* Jungschulz

- 5th Cossack Regiment of the Don (*Don Kosaken Reiter-Rgt.5*), under the orders of the *Oberstleutnant* Kononov

- 6th Cossack Regiment of the Terek (*Terek-Kosaken Reiter-Rgt.6*), under the orders of the *Oberstleutnant* von Knalben

Each of these regiments (2,000 men of which 160 Germans) was divided into six squadrons which in turn were divided into two groups of 12 cavalrymen. However, due to the lack of horses, some groups of the 2nd Siberian Cossack Regiment were equipped with bicycles. The two brigades also included a heavy squadron equipped with 8 80mm mortars and 8 heavy machine guns.

Kosaken-Regiment 6 was not a cavalry unit, but an infantry unit (*Plastun*, according to Cossack terminology). The unit was created by Captain Ewert von Renteln. German-Baltic from Estonia, born on April 11, 1893 in Gut-Bremerfeld, Renteln had served in the Czar's mounted guard, when the Baltic countries were part of the Russian Empire. Stripped of his possessions and then deported to Siberia during the civil war, he managed to escape and return to Estonia, fighting in a Franco-German free corps against the Communists. In August 1941, he enlisted in the *Wehrmacht* as a mere volunteer. Promoted to officer, he obtained both classes of the Iron Cross on June 4 and September 23, 1942.

The Axis Forces

Oberstleutnant **Werner Jungschulz.**

In addition to these two brigades, the division included a reconnaissance company entirely made up of German personnel, two groups of horse artillery (one of the Don Cossacks and one of the Kuban) comprising a total of six batteries (with about 200 men per battery), one anti-tank squadron with five 50mm guns, a pioneer battalion and several other support units, all numbered 55. Also worth mentioning is the existence of a reserve and training regiment (*Freiw Lehr-und-Ersatz-Regiment*), with a force of around 10-15,000 men, under the orders of the Oberst von Bosse, with the command post in Mokowo. This unit was joined by the Cossack cadet school, a sort of cadet corps comprising Cossack orphans aged between 14 and 18, adopted by the division. Among them was Boris Nabakov, a young orphan from the Feodosia region and an adopted son of Pannwitz.

Transfer to Croatia

Initially engaged on the Eastern front, Pannwitz's unit was finally transferred to Croatia to be committed against the partisans. This transfer was part of Hitler's decision in autumn 1943 to transfer all Osttruppen to the western front. Shortly before the departure of the division, Pannwitz sent General Krasnov and then General Naumenko, an old ataman of the Kuban Cossacks, to Mielau. At Pannwitz's request, Krasnov reviewed the division, then delivered a speech to explain to the Cossacks that fighting in the Balkans against the communist resistance was as important as fighting on the Eastern front. Krasnov's words served to reassure the Cossacks about their future. The first Cossack convoys left Mielau in mid-September 1943. After passing through Poland, Slovakia and Hungary, they arrived in Yugoslavia. Here, the division was aggregated to the *2.Pz.Armee* of *Generaloberst* Lothar Rendulic, in turn dependent on the Army Group E of *Generalfeldmarschall* Freiherr von Weichs. It was ordered to be stationed in Serbia, between Novi-Sad and Belgrade, northeast of the Kukujevci-Mitrovica-Ruma-Indja-Belgrade line. The command post was

Cossack volunteers on a river, 1943.

installed in Mitrovica. Immediately after his arrival, *Generalmajor* von Pannwitz, accompanied by *Oberst* von Schultz, went to the command of the group of armies in Belgrade, then to that of the *2.Pz.Armee* in Banjska and later to the various general staffs of the sector, always receiving a cold welcome from officers who did not believe in the effectiveness of a cavalry unit. But soon they changed their mind.

Croatia, Winter 1943-44: a Cossack volunteer. Observation of a main road.

Croatia, Winter 1943-44: a Cossack volunteer in a farm.

In early October 1943, the two Cossack brigades were engaged in a first operation against the partisans in the Fruska Gora region, between the assembly area of the division and the southern bank of the Danube (south-west of Novi-Sad). This operation was not successful because the partisans, following their tactics, withdrew avoiding to clash with the Cossacks. A second operation was launched shortly afterwards in the confluence of the Sava and Drina rivers, south-west of Mitrovica, but once again without great results, except to allow the

Cossacks to familiarize themselves with the terrain and methods of war of the partisan gangs. In the meantime, since his arrival in Croatia, *Generalmajor* von Pannwitz had to face numerous problems concerning his units, first of all the continuous infringements of discipline by the Cossacks. Some of them were guilty of violent acts against the civilian population. In addition, Tito's communists attempted to destabilize the morale of the division by infiltrating their agents to attempt to induce the Cossacks to desertion.

Cossack volunteers moving through dense woodland in Croatia, Winter 1943-44.

A Cossack second-lieutnant, wearing a white fur *Kubanka*, talking to German officers.

A group of horsemen in Croatia, 1943.

But these attempts had no effect: despite the worsening military situation, the number of desertions within the Cossack units remained very low. From their arrival in Yugoslavia until the end of the war, only 250 cases of desertion occurred.

In mid-October, the Cossack division was transferred to Croatia west of the Vukovar-Vinkovci-Vrpolje line, with the mission of protecting the communication lines and above all the Zagreb-Belgrade railway line, a vital artery for the supply of German troops who operated in the Balkans and which were continuously attacked by partisan gangs.

Cossack horsemen of the 4th Kuban Regiment, during an anti-partisan operation in Croatia.

The Cossack units carried out this mission successfully, with patrols along the entire railway line and along the other communication lines, also organizing coups d'état within the territories controlled by the partisans.

New operations

In late November, despite von Pannwitz's opposition, the two brigades of the division were assigned to two different sectors. The 1st Brigade of Oberst von Wolff was transferred to the Sisak-Petrinja-Glina and Sisak-Sanja-Kostjanica region (south-east of Zagreb), where it took over from the SS *Nordland* division. Since its arrival in this sector, the 2nd Cossack Regiment of Siberia, under the orders of *Oberstleutnant* von Nolcken, had been severely committed against the partisans in the Petrinja sector. The fighting continued to retake the region of Glina where the partisans acted freely. In the course of these operations, the Cossacks recaptured the farms and villages occupied by the partisans. The 2nd Brigade of Oberst Wagner, was attached to the *XV.Geb.Korps* to be engaged in the Derventa-Doboj-Gracanica area, in the Bosnian mountains north of Zenica, with the mission of controlling the lines of communication in the direction of Sarajevo. Constantly engaged in these security operations, Oberst Wagner's men successfully faced the partisan gangs, despite the difficulties of the terrain. At the end of 1943 and following these first jobs, the Germans had a precise idea regarding the military value of the Cossack units. In January 1944, some unit commanders were replaced. *Oberst* von Wolff, commander of the 1st Brigade, was replaced by *Oberst* von Bosse, while the command of the 2nd Brigade was replaced by *Oberst* von Schultz.

Croatia, Winter 1943-44: members of the 2nd Siberian Cossack Regiment receiving decorations from General von Pannwitz.

Von Pannwitz exchanges a few word.

At the 1st Cossack Regiment of the Don, *Oberst* Wagner replaced *Oberstleutnant* Graff zu Dohna and at the 3rd Kuban Regiment, *Oberstleutnant* Lehmann replaced *Oberstleutnant* Jungschulz. In mid-January, the 2nd Brigade left Bosnia and returned to join the 1st Brigade, located on a line that went from the area south-east of Zagreb to Jastrebarsko-Karlovac.

On March 29, 1944, the 2nd Siberia Rregiment under Oberst von Nolcken, reinforced by Captain Weil's recon squadron, managed to engage in combat in the Dubravcak region, north of Sisak, a brigade of partisans with a strength of 400 men. The partisan brigade was completely annihilated, but at the cost of heavy losses: two officers, *Oberleutnant* Von Amelung and Leutnant von Flotow, eight non-commissioned officers and soldiers of the German liaison unit, a Cossack officer and twenty non-commissioned officers and Cossack soldiers. After this action, the Cossack division was first mentioned in an official *Wehrmacht* statement.

Croatia, early 1944: a group of Cossacks moving through a village suspected of partisan activities.

Along the Zagreb-Belgrad railway line, 1944.

In April 1944, after the Easter holidays, the 1st Brigade participated in a vast operation against the partisans entrenched in the sector of Karlovac, subordinate to the *2.Pz.Armee*, together with Croatian elements and Ustasha units. In early May, the division staff and the 2nd Brigade were deployed to Nova-Gradiska. The 1st Brigade of *Oberst* von Bosse moved south of Sace, on the Zagreb-Sisak-Sunja-Kostajnica-Brod line. The Cossacks managed to completely pacify this area after a series of energetic reconnaissance actions and roundups. During the same period, the 1st Brigade participated in the *'Scach'* operation, with an attack along the Glina-Topusko line: the partisans avoided fighting in the open field and the Cossack regiments returned to their starting bases. However, during the retreat, the 2nd Cossack Regiment of Siberia found itself completely surrounded by partisans. The Cossack unit eventually managed to free itself thanks to the intervention of elements of the *369. Infanterie-Division*, the famous *'Devil'* division, made up of Croatian volunteers. On June 29, Pannwitz launched an extensive operation with the 3rd and 5th regiments of the 2nd Brigade. Starting from the Pozega valley, the Cossacks marched to Dakovo through the Papuk mountains.

Cossack horsemen, guarding the Zagreb-Belgrad railway line, 1944.

The partisans avoided fighting by falling back to the north and east. However, the 3rd Cossack Regiment of the Kuban under *Oberstleutnant* Lehmann Kuban was engaged against a strong partisan unity between Rusevo and Levanjska-Varos, east of Pleternica. After a furious hand-to-hand combat, under the energetic command of *Hauptmann* Langfeld and *Hauptmann* Kreide, the Cossacks inflicted heavy losses on the partisans. On July 10, 1944, the 1st Brigade participated in another major operation south-west of Zagreb in the Metlika sector and on the Uskoks mountains. During these actions the Cossacks, despite facing for the first time well-led and well-equipped units, behaved very well. On July 15, the three regiments of the brigade carried out a concentric attack crowned with success and which resolved on July 16 with the conquest of Metlika. Shortly after this operation, new changes of command occurred within the division. *Oberst* von Baath passed to the command of the 1st Brigade. *Oberstleutnant* von Klein passed to the command of the 4th Cossack Regiment of the Kuban. Between 25 and 26 July, the 3rd and 5th regiments of the 2nd Brigade were engaged in a vast round-up in Bosnia. The two regiments progressed towards Cerovoca-Prnjavor. But, once again, the partisans disappeared and the Cossacks failed to achieve concrete results. Only the 2nd Squadron of the 5th Cossack Regiment of the Don, under the orders of Major Borissov, on 2 August, managed to intercept a group of partisans, inflicting however only minor losses.

(To be continued)

Bibliography
Massimiliano Afiero, "*I volontari stranieri di Hitler*", Ritter edizioni
Francois de Lannoy, "*Les cosacques de Pannwitz*", Editions Heimdal
D. Littlejohn, "*Foreign Legion of the Third Reich, Vol. 4*", R. Bender Publishing
Erich Kern, "*I Cosacchi di Hitler*", Ritter edizioni

Hans Siegel
Knight's Cross Holder of the 12. SS-Panzer Division
by Peter Mooney

Born in Bockau on the 25th of July 1918, he was a member of the *Hitler Jugend* from April 1933 through to early-January 1936. He entered the *SS* (with SS number 293 261) on the 6th of January 1936 and was placed with the *6. SS-Totenkopf Standarte,* but also served with the *15. SS-Standarte* until April 1938. He moved to the *R.A.D.* from April to October, then at the beginning of November, he moved to the *Leibstandarte*.

Two photos of Hans Siegel, early in his SS career 1936, with the *15. SS-Standarte*.

A *Leibstandarte* StuG.III, Summer 1940.

He held the Reichs Sports Badge in Bronze pre-war. He took part in the Polish campaign as part of the 12. Kompanie's mortar team. He was sent for officer training at Bad Tolz from the beginning of November 1939 through to late-February 1940. When he returned to the *Leibstandarte,* it was with their *4. Kompanie*, within their Replacement Battalion. He was promoted to *SS-Untersturmführer* at the start of August 1940. In 1941, he attended a training course for heavy weapons and following that, became a Platoon Commander in the youthful *Sturmgeschutze* Battalion. On the 9th of November 1942, he was promoted to *SS-Obersturmführer*.

Hans Siegel getting ready to depart on a train journey, behind him, a short barrelled *Stug*.   **Waffen-SS grenadiers and *StuG.III* on the Kharkov Front, February 1943.**

On the 18th of February 1943 (during the Kharkov fighting), he was awarded the Second Class Iron Cross. There are frequently used images from this battle, seen in many books, that show Hans Siegel with his *Sturmgeschutze* being re-armed from halftracks, plus Siegel himself destroying Soviet anti-tank guns with rifle granades.

German *Sturmgeschütz* on the Kharkov Front, February-March 1943.

The award of the Russian Front Medal was made on the 6th of February 1943, the Tank Assault Badge and the Wound Badge in Silver were both awarded on the 30th of March; that wound badge was for severe wounds suffered to his spine, which resulted in him being removed from the frontline for treatment, but then later, being declared unfit for military duty. In the second half of 1943, *SS-Ostuf.* Hans Siegel was placed with the SS-Training and Replacement Battalion.

Siegel and Kameraden around one of their vehicles which drove over a mine, 1943.

Siegel and Kameraden inspecting some of the mines discovered in the area, 1943.

Hans Siegel prepares to blow up a Russian 45mm PaK gun with a small demolition charge.

Hans Siegel and his comrades duck for cover as the demolition charge he placed in the captured Soviet 45 mm anti tank explode, February 1943.

His next posting, was with the *12. SS-Panzer Division 'Hitlerjugend'*, from mid-January 1944, given the role of *8. Kompanie* Commander within their Panzer Regiment.

The award of the First Class Iron Cross came on the 14th of June, with promotion to *SS-Hauptsturmführer* coming one week later.

His armoured vehicle was hit by enemy fire on the 27th of June 1944, which gave him severe burns to his hands and face; those were his fifth wound. He insisted that he remain with the Division.

SS-Hstuf. **Hans Siegel, showing his *Ritterkreuz*.**

A *Hitlerjugend PzKpfw.IV* in Normady, June 1944.

Ritterkreuz

At the start of July, *SS-Obersturmbannführer* (Hanreich) penned the document which, asked for the award of the Knight's Cross for Siegel, it contained:

"SS-Hauptsturmführer Siegel is the attack mover of his Battalion. He destroyed, during the eventful offensive and defensive battles for Caen, as Kompanie Commander, 37 enemy tanks through his Kompanie; he alone destroyed 11 enemy tanks.

On the 11.6.1944 he must, because of the fourth occasion of being shot up, launch a counter-attack eastwards of Tilly, reaching out far ahead of their own lines and even brought in prisoners.

On the 27.6.1944 the English broke through Cheux from Grainville and Monen with tanks and armoured cars. Siegel struggled from severely depleted defences, with them destroying enemy tanks at a distance of 30 metres. Evading the new enemy, he went in a night-time attack, north of this area and won new ground to prevent the breakthrough of the enemy tanks upon Grainville and to the south. Siegel held his positions without any infantry protection and despite the heaviest artillery barrages. When preparing and committing his men in the dark of the night, he was surprised by an enemy reconnaissance troop. In the ensuing scuffle, he suffered a stab wound to his right side. Nevertheless, he successfully resisted the enemy and retained his position. The next morning the enemy attacked again. Siegel fought until the last of his tanks, when he pulled together new forces and once again prevented a breakthrough of the Englishmen to their rear. Siegel was wounded for the fifth time, after his tank was shot up, suffering severe burns".

A *Hitlerjugend PzKpfw.IV* in Normady, June 1944.

Hans Siegel autographed image.

SS-Hauptsturmführer **Hans Siegel.**

SS-Standartenführer and Divisional Commander, Kurt Meyer, endorsed this award, adding his thoughts on the worthiness of Hans Siegel to be a bearer of the medal, due to his special, brave deeds. His Korps Commander, Sepp Dietrich, also added an endorsement of the outstandingly brave acts of Siegel; this overall proposal was approved on the 23rd of August 1944.

After receiving treatment near the front, he returned to service and was placed in command of the II. Battalion, *SS-Panzer Regiment 12*. His unit was refitted at Fallingbostel from November and as there were insufficient tanks to equip his Battalion, they did not participate in the Ardennes fighting. Siegel himself returned to the front line on the 10th of January 1945, at a time when the *I. Battalion* was being held back as a temporary reserve.

Hans Siegel and *12. SS-Pz.Rgt.* **Kameraden** visiting *Reichswirtschaftminister* **Funk in Berlin.**

Hans Siegel and the *Panzertruppen* of *Hitlerjugend* at Fallingbostel camp, Autumn 1944.

His first orders were to scour the combat area and recover and serviceable tanks for repair. By the end of January, the remnants of the *12. SS* were moving back into Germany and beginning their onwards move towards Hungary. During that fighting, in late-March 1945, Siegel was wounded further (ninth wound) and moved to hospital. He returned to his men at the earliest opportunity and fought further against the Russian juggernaut. He was promoted to *SS-Sturmbannführer* in April 1945. A further heavy wound was inflicted on the 8th of May 1945, which destroyed the elbow on his left arm. He was captured by the Russians, who treated him, but they had to amputate the arm. He returned from Russian captivity and initially lived in Austria, before moving to Germany. He was active in the veterans associations, but also in helping to educate new generations, which included close links with the Canadian military – his former enemy. The author was lucky enough to meet Herr Siegel on a few occasions at the *I. SS-Panzer Korps* veteran's association; he was an energetic and very friendly man.

Other photos of Hans Siegel and his men at Fallingbostel camp in Autumn 1944.

Hans Siegel and myself, 2000.

The very visual result of his end of May 1945 wound was there for all to see, but that certainly did not prevent him from signing various photos and books for the eager people waiting. He died on the 18th of April 2002, in Andernach.

Bibliography
Waffen-SS Knights and Their Battles – Volume 5 (June to August 1944): Peter Mooney. (release date to be confirmed)

Personal discussions and correspondence with Hans Siegel and myself (1999 – 2001)

SS-Panzergrenadier-Division Wiking on the Manytsch Front and the withdrawal to Rostov, January 1943

by Massimiliano Afiero

SS-Ostubaf. Max Schäfer, with his men.

A *T-34* tank knocked out by SS engineers at close range.

At the beginning of January 1943, the *Wiking* was engaged in a series of defensive battles along the Manytsch River, where SS-Gruf. Steiner had set up a line of defence. During the retreat from the Caucasus, the SS engineers were heavily engaged in combat, as were the grenadiers. Since the beginning of the campaign on the Eastern Front, they had always found themselves in the front lines, to cross rivers, to attack tanks with magnetic mines, to blow up bunkers. The unit commander was always where his men were, setting explosives under enemy fire. SS-Stubaf. Schäfer, a native of Karlsruhe, had celebrated his thirty-sixth birthday on one of the coldest days in January, along with his engineers. More than anyone else, Schäfer had learned perfectly the technique of withdrawal; if the unit pulled out too quickly, the enemy could easily surround his comrades. If he pulled out too late, he ran the risk of being captured. No one was better than Schäfer at performing that maneouver. When their turn came, the engineers clung to their positions to slow down the advance of the soviet troops who had been thrown in

The Axis Forces

pursuit of the retreating German troops. The Soviet infantry were preceded by relays of *T-34* tanks which ran over all of the defences, destroying everyone and everything beneath their tracks. The men who were scattered over the snowy ground were fired on by the machine guns aboard the tanks. Each attack ended up in a slaughter.

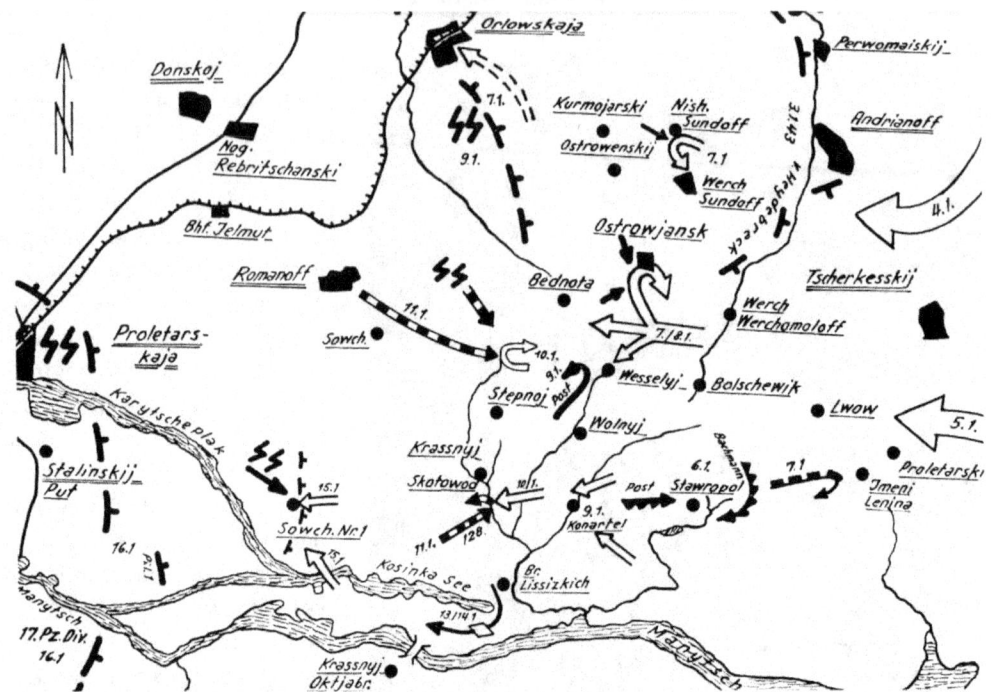

Operational sector of *Wiking* units during the first half of January 1943.

German engineers inspecting a knocked-out enemy tank.

The engineers of the companies of Schäfer's battalion had no anti-tank weapons available to ward off the tanks. So, they attacked the T-34s at close range, placing mines underneath the tracks or attaching magnetic hollow charge explosives to the turrets. In either case, these were very dangerous actions. The enemy tanks had to be approached by taking advantage of blind spots, while other comrades kept the accompanying infantry at bay. They let the tanks get to within a few meters, jumped from their holes, placed the mines or charges and then rolled away as quickly as possible from the blast. Many lost their lives in that unequal battle. Their bodies lay close to their victims, lifeless in the snow. When his men attacked the tanks, *SS-Stubaf.* Schäfer went to the front line himself, to the totally isolated forward posts. Max Schäfer would appear unexpectedly riding in his vehicle. He issued orders, picked up the wounded and reassured the survivors. *"Hang on a little longer. We'll be out of this soon"*.

An SS soldier observing the movement of enemy on the road, January 1943.

An *MG-34* on a heavy tripod, in a defensive position.

Thanks to Schäfer, who was known throughout the *Wiking* division as *"Macki"*, a number of critical situations were been resolved. During the rapid withdrawals, the SS engineers were used to organize new defensive positions a few kilometers to the west.

The withdrawal to Rostov

The long march towards Rostov continued, each day more exhausting and bloody. The division's columns left a trail of abandoned vehicles and corpses behind them. The survivors continued to fight day and night. Around mid-January 1943, two companies of the *Wiking* engineer battalion were assembled in an area where the troops that were coming from the Caucasus could rest for a few hours. For the first time, after many weeks, the engineers were moved to the rear area. The engineers then busied themselves with cleaning their weapons, salvaging equipment, mines, explosives, hollow charges and other material. *SS-Stubaf*. Schäfer himself reported in to the division headquarters. In the middle of the night, gunfire was heard: *"The Russians! Alarm! Everybody out!"*.

A Soviet tank destroyed on the outskirts of a village, January 1943.

A German mortar in position to support a counterattack.

The Soviets had been able to pass through the German lines with the aid of darkness and in the midst of a snowstorm. Quickly, the two engineer company commanders realized that they were being attacked by vastly superior enemy forces. *"It's at least a regiment"*. The engineers had to fight against odds of ten to one. And the Soviet infantry were supported by heavy weapons. Mortar rounds could be heard falling in the village. The engineers sprang to action and began to reply to the enemy fire by the light from the first burning houses. To the west, the road still seemed open. The Soviets had not yet competed surrounding the village. Messengers were soon sent to request assistance. They disappeared into the night. The engineers had to wait, and meanwhile they fired between the burning isbas, trying not to give up any ground. If the enemy infantry managed to break through, there would have been hand-to-hand fighting and they knew that they were greatly outnumbered. The Soviets continued to get closer. Grenades were tossed. The enemy was now only a few dozen meters away. Suddenly the sound of an engine was heard coming from the west.

Waffen-SS engineers moving between the isbas of a burning village, January 1943..

Waffen-SS soldiers and a knocked-out tank, January 1943.

During the night, a vehicle appeared. On board was the engineer commander, Max Schäfer. He had arrived just when all seemed lost. Climbing out of his vehicle, he went quickly to his command post.

"What's facing us?", he asked his NCOs.

"At least a regiment", they responded.

"Do they have tanks too?", he asked further.

"None that we can see right now", was the reply.

SS-Stubaf. Schäfer didn't hesitate an instant before issuing new orders: "...*No problem if we have to fight ten to one. It doesn't matter, the important thing is that we don't have any tanks to deal with. We'll counter-attack*".

The survivors of the two engineer companies understood that this desperate action was their only chance. Only those of them who did not die in the fighting would escape from that hell. This time, however, it would be a lot tougher than other times.

There were about three hundred engineers who sprang forward, shouting and yelling. In the midst of those men, machine pistol in hand and a cigar in his mouth was old "*Macki*". The action was really noisy. According to the official report issued after the fighting, about seven hundred dead Soviet soldiers were counted and two hundred prisoners taken, not counting the weapons captured and equipment destroyed. For *SS-Stubaf.* Schäfer this was only one stage of the lengthy withdrawal. He knew that there was still much for his engineers to do: defend the final positions of the bridgehead in front of Rostov to allow all of the *Wiking* units to cross the river and to escape capture.

German troops crossing a bridge, January 1943.

SS-*Ostubaf.* Max Schäfer.

And so, yet again, the engineers became infantrymen. During the following nights the Soviets attacked, taking advantage of snow storms. Every breach that was made in the defensive line was plugged. The bridgehead was defended to the last. *SS-Stubaf.* Schäfer gathered the survivors of his battalion and once again threw them into a wild counter-attack. It was either folly or dangerous shrewdness. To remain in place would have meant letting themselves be killed. By attacking, the enemy was taken by surprise. The engineer commander played his cards well. The engineers held fast, and the *Wiking* columns were able to withdraw slowly under the protection of their rifles and their mines.

The Knight's Cross for Max Schäfer

For the defence of the Stalinski-Put position, *SS-Stubaf.* Max Schäfer was awarded the Knight's Cross on 12 February 1943. A few weeks before, on 30 January 1943, he had been promoted to the rank of *SS-Obersturmbannführer*.

The Axis Forces

A *Waffen-SS* soldier armed with an *MP-40*.

SS-Ostubaf. Manfred Schönfelder.

The award was presented personally by the *Wiking* commander, *SS-Gruf.* Steiner, during an official ceremony at Krasno-Armeiskoje. Following is the text of the citation, as reported in official documentation: *"...SS-Stubaf. Schäfer was deployed with his battalion over a wide defensive front, on the bridgehead southeast of Proletarskaja. During the night of 19.1.1943, in a snowstorm and with the ground turned into a quagmire, the bridgehead was attacked and flanked from the east by a large enemy force. A bridge situated on the Manytsch River, over which the Proletarskaja-Seelekgeführdot railway line also crossed was ready to be destroyed, and suddenly became the only escape route for the division from the Proletarskaja bridgehead. SS-Stubaf. Schäfer quickly realized that the division risked being trapped, and so on his own initiative he went to the forefront of his battalion and despite the difficulties caused by the snow, launched a counterattack to counter the enemy's attempt at encirclement. The violent fighting that ensued stalled the enemy advance and attempted encirclement. This action prevented the division from being surrounded and blocked to the north by the Manytsch River and made possible the evacuation of the division in a regular and orderly fashion...".*

On 12 January 1943, the *Westland* regiment lost its commander, *SS-Ostubaf.* Harry Polewacz, a Berliner, who would have turned thirty in a few weeks, who fell during the rear guard fighting, hit by a Soviet sniper. On 23 December 1942 he had been awarded the Knight's Cross as *Sturmbannfüher und Kommandeur of III./Nordland*. SS-Stubaf. Hajo von Hadeln, commander of *I./Westland*, also was killed, struck by a shell fragment during a Soviet artillery bombardment. The death of Polewacz, during the full retreat, just at the time the division was going through a difficult period, was a real catastrophe. To replace him at the head of the regiment, *SS-Gruf.* Steiner designated his chief of staff, *SS-Hstuf.* Günther Sitter. The post of *Wiking* chief of staff was assumed by *SS-Hstuf.* Manfred Schönfelder, who would hold that position until the end of the war.

SS-Stubaf. **Hans Lohmann.**

The Proletarskaja bridgehead

The *Wiking* grenadier regiments, often reduced to the strength of a large company, established defensive positions in isolated villages in order to cover the retreat. As the *Westland* had fought at Simonviki and the *Germania* at Baljabanov, the *Nordland* had dug in at Proletarskaja, on the Manytsch, where the *LVII.Armee-Korps* had established a bridgehead. Holding this position was of vital importance to keep a crossing over the Don open between Rostov and Bataisk. In addition to *Wiking* units, the *23.Pz.Div.* and *17.Pz.Div.* were also in the area. *I./Nordland*, commanded by *SS-Stubaf.* Lohmann, had since 13 January been dug into the village Krasnoje-Snamja. At dawn on 14 January, the Soviets attacked the position with six *T-34* tanks, supported by hundreds of infantrymen dressed completely in white. The SS grenadiers had no anti-tank weapons and were forced to seek shelter in the houses, leaving the streets free for the enemy tanks. The Germanic volunteers could deal only with the infantry. *SS-Stubaf.* Lohmann made his men fall back halfway through the village, behind an improvised minefield. The Soviet tanks had in the meantime come to a halt. Some of the volunteers decided to blow them up with hollow charges.

A formation of Soviet tanks on the attack, January 1943.

An SS soldier moved behind the houses, jumped behind the turret of a *T-34* and placed a mine. Then he jumped to the ground to take cover. Unfortunately the attachments for the mine did not hold and the charge fell, exploding in the snow, without causing any damage to the enemy tank. Falling back, the Germanic volunteers soon reached the battalion aid station which suddenly found itself in the front line.

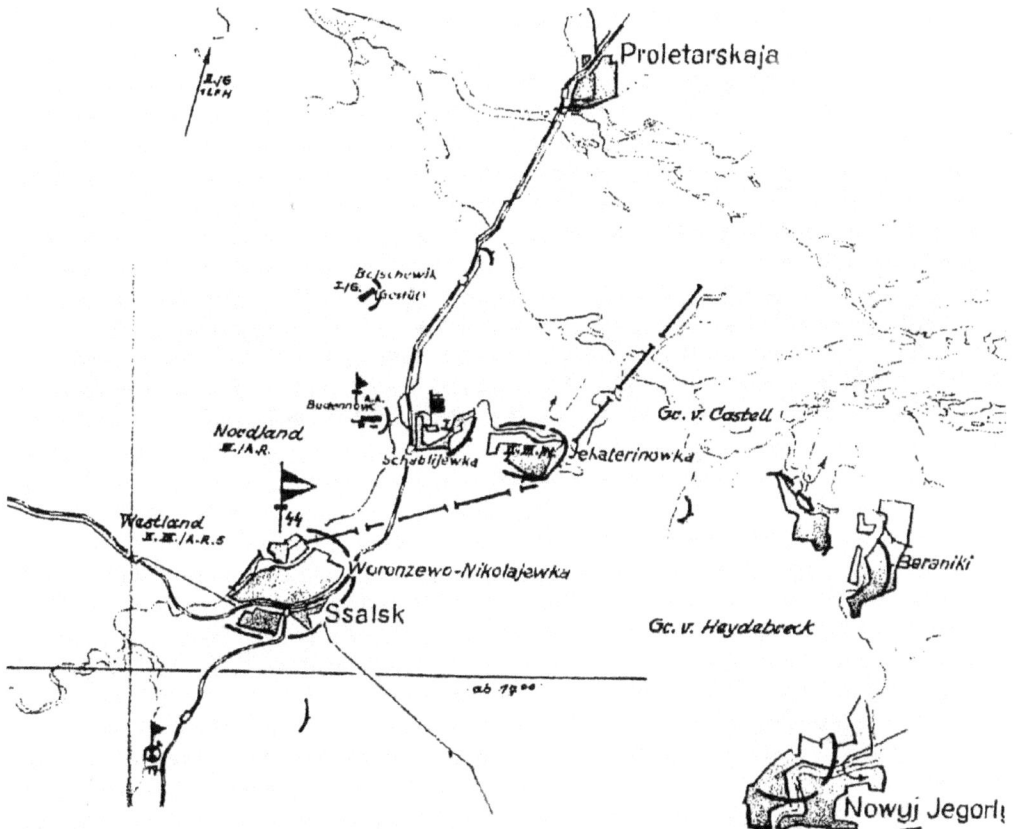

Situation of *Wiking* units north of Salsk, January 1943.

SS soldiers and a knocked-out tank.

"*It's full of wounded comrades here. You can't abandon them!*" shouted a doctor. And then, it was decided to counter-attack yet again. The *Nordland* grenadiers wrested several dozen meters of ground from the enemy to protect their aid station. *SS-Stubaf.* Lohmann still had a telephone available and requested aid from the regiment. "*We are being attacked by tanks!*". At that very moment a *T-34* passed in front of the battalion command post and the window was open. At the other end of the phone line *SS-Ostubaf.* Jörchel was able to appreciate the real extent of the danger and quickly sent *SS-Stubaf.* Stoffers' grenadiers towards Krasnoje-Snamja. The reinforcements arrived during the night and quickly joined in a new counter-attack that was able to oust the Soviets from the village.

Wiking **vehicles destroyed by Soviet aircraft, January 1943** (*Charles Trang Collection*).

SS-Brigadeführer **Herbert-Otto Gille.**

At dawn the following day, the T-34s returned to attack Lohmann's and Stoffers' soldiers and were again driven back towards the centre of the village. Then Collani's Finnish volunteers and four assault guns arrived, which played a decisive role in the battle. A fresh counter-attack by the SS units enabled the entire village to be recaptured. After a few hours the Soviets returned to attack, despite the heavy losses they had suffered. This time, however, thanks to the supporting fire of the assault guns their attack was thrown back.

The battle for Jekaterinovka

During the night of 19 January 1943, some Soviet units ventured out onto the ice of the Manytsch River and were able to break into the village of Jekaterinovka. This place was a pass-through point for the *Wiking* division which was retreating from the Proletarskaja area. It was unpleasant news that reached *SS-Brigadeführer* Gille, who had assumed temporary command of the division: *"We risk being cut off. We must hold on to the crossing over the Manytsch at all costs"*, he said to *SS-Stubaf.* Schönfelder. The road that led from Proletarskaja to Ssalk had to remain clear to continue the withdrawal. It was thus necessary for combat units to be committed to secure the sector.

SS troops during fighting to defend a village, January 1943.

Hans-Joachim Porsch.

SS-*Ostubaf.* Hans Collani.

"...Only the Finns can be committed", stated Schönfelder.

"...Exactly, I was thinking of using them", agreed Gille.

SS-Stubaf. Collani's battalion was in reserve at that moment. The *II./Nordland* was to replace it. The relief movement took place at night and the Finnish volunteers left Proletarskaja for Schlabijevka, where they arrived at two in the morning. At dawn, the *10.Kompanie* under *SS-Ostuf.* Porsch and *11.Kompanie* under *SS-Ostuf.* Deck reached the jump-off positions for the attack. This time, *9.Kompanie* under *SS-Ostuf.* Ertel, remained in reserve, ready to support the attack. There were about a thousand Soviets inside Jekaterinovka, backed up by guns and mortars. *"We will attack at precisely nine o'clock"* Collani announced to his adjutant Hirt. He had only two companies available, but had managed to get some reinforcements. To the left, Porsch's *10.Kompanie* would be supported by a *Panzer* and two assault guns; to the right, Deck's *11.Kompanie* was to be supported by two panzers and a single assault gun. After having gathered around the tanks, the Finnish grenadiers advanced towards Jekaterinovka. The Finns knew that they had to open the road not only for the *Nordland* regiment but for the entire *Wiking*. They had to clear the enemy roadblock along the road to Salsk. Everything was going well. Despite the long march from the Caucasus, they had maintained their offensive, almost savage, spirit, which never ceased to amaze the Germans. After about a quarter of an hour of fighting, well supported by the assault guns, the point elements reached the stream that separated the village of Jekaterinovka in two.

Finnish volunteers engaged in fighting at Jekaterinovka, January 1943.

An *MG-34* mounted on a *StuG.III Ausf.G*.

But there was still much to do. They had to move to the north and take the houses occupied by Soviet soldiers, one after another. *SS-Ostuf.* Porsch and the men of *10.Kompanie* advanced for about eight hundred meters without encountering any difficulties. Taken by surprise, the Soviets fell back but did not give up. To the contrary, they reacted by barricading themselves in houses. They had to be routed out using hand grenades and engaging in fierce hand-to-hand fighting. The Finnish volunteers fought with daggers and bayonets. Porsch had never seen his men fight with such determination and resolve. But shortly before ten in the morning the Soviet defense stiffened further and Porsch's men were stalled by a massive artillery shelling. *SS-Ostuf.* Porsch then tried to assess the situation: half of the village of Jekaterinovka had been captured. On the right, Deck's *11.Kompanie* had performed outstandingly. Everything would have gone well if the Soviets had not brought in fresh reinforcements. The two Finnish companies, which together totalled only about a hundred men, found themselves facing about a thousand enemy infantry, supported by many heavy weapons and artillery. At that same time, *SS-Ostuf.* Porsch was mortally wounded by an enemy bullet to the head. Command of the company was assumed by *SS-Ostuf.* Tauno Pohjanlehto. That Finnish officer had from the beginning of the campaign on the Eastern Front earned a good reputation as an assault combatant, especially during the fighting on Hill 701 at Malgobeck.

A Finnish volunteer in a defensive position with an *MG-34*, January 1943.

Finnish volunteers. Note the *"pukko"* carried by the soldier on the right (O.W.).

The Finnish volunteers gathered around the fellow countryman and commander, ready to go on the attack. To their right, even their comrades of *11.Kompanie* had been stopped by the enemy fire. At the same time, fresh reinforcements were joining the enemy; many Soviet infantrymen suddenly poured out of the Kolhkoz, trying to encircle and surround the Finns. *SS-Stubaf.* Collani quickly realized the danger and sent several engineers from his heavy company as reinforcements. At that moment he could do no more, deciding to keep Ertel's company still in reserve. Soon after, about six hundred Soviet infantry counter-attacked in an attempt to overwhelm the two Finnish companies inside Jekaterinovka. Pohjanlehto's company was particularly threatened. *"Let them get closer"* he ordered his men. Machine gun bursts temporarily stalled the Soviets, but there were so many of them that in the end they were able to break through, making contact with the first of the Finish positions. Hand-to-hand fighting ensued, during which the Finnish volunteers used their daggers (the famous "*pukko*"). The enemy counter-attack was driven off. "*It's our turn now*" Pohjanlehto shouted to his men.

A *Nordland MG-34* in a defensive position, January 1943 (*Geir Brenden Collection*).

A *Waffen-SS* 75mm *le.IG.18* in position, January 1943.

The Finnish volunteers threw themselves forward like devils unleashed. After having overrun the mass of enemy infantry, they reached a heavy mortar position, killing all of the crew with knives and hand grenades. The enemy mortars were quickly used to provide supporting fire for their comrades, enabling Deck's grenadiers to stabilize their positions. The Soviets attacked again, bringing in new reserves. There was a *Wiking* artillery observer with the Finns. Providing information to his comrades via radio, it was possible to hit the attacking Soviet infantry. At the same time, the machine guns of *10* and *11.Kompanie* let loose a torrent of fire.

SS-Ostuf. **Tauno Pohjanlehto.**

The Soviets fell back, but the Finns also suffered heavy losses. Around noontime, Collani was forced to throw the remaining engineers of *12.Kompanie* into the fray. After about half an hour, the Soviets again attacked the battalion's positions with all of their available forces. Pohjanlehto and Deck counted almost four hundred enemy infantry closing in on them. The attack was thrown back with great sacrifice and cost in casualties. New reinforcements for the Finns consisted only of a *Wehrmacht* engineer platoon. There were no further enemy attacks into the night. More than three hundred Soviet soldiers lay dead in front of the Finnish positions and at least a hundred prisoners had been captured by Collani's battalion. Also captured were about a dozen anti-tank rifles, two heavy machine guns, six mortars and many sub-machine guns. However, the battle was not yet over. During the night, the Soviets brought in new reinforcements. *SS-Stubaf*. Collani then decided to launch a counter-attack, with the *9* and *11.Kompanie*, to beat the enemy and take him by surprise. At dawn on 20 January, *SS-Ostuf*. Pohjanlehto formed an assault group that included some grenadiers from the two companies and the engineer group commanded by *SS-Uscha*. Toivo Vaino.

Finnish volunteers fighting at Jekaterinovka, January 1943, with the support of a *Panzer III*.

January 1943: a well-armed group of Finnish volunteers. There seems to be no lack of hand grenades (*Olli Wikberg*).

Attached to them were the medic Valtonen and two liaison officers, one German and a Swede from Finland. In all, there were about a dozen men. *SS-Ostuf.* Pohjanlehto loved to lead these small patrols. The guns of the artillery regiment supported the attack. The SS grenadiers moved towards the eastern part of the village. Two panzers were on the road, halting every so often to fire. The nearest houses occupied by the enemy were attacked with hand grenades. The Soviets were taken by surprise once again; they felt that the Finns were exhausted but instead saw them pop up in front of them. Most of the Soviet soldiers consisted of young recruits without much experience. Instead of coming out and fighting, they continued to hide in the houses. The panzers hit them one after another, showing no pity. *SS-Ostuf.* Pohjanlehto led the attack like a madman and his men acted likewise. It was a band of raging devils going from house to house throwing grenades, shooting and yelling. There was no time to lose, the enemy could not be given any breathing room. Pohkanlehto continued to tell his men: "..*Keep moving forward, move more quickly*". Some Soviet soldiers emerged from the houses and cellars with their hands in the air. They surrendered. They did not know that they had been attacked by only about a dozen men. There were only six of them left when they reached the end of the village. Leading them was *SS-Ostuf.* Pohjanlehto. Had the others been killed or wounded? No, they had stayed behind to collect and disarm the captured enemy soldiers. Then a heavy machine gun was emplaced to face any enemy attack against the village. The village of Jekaterinovka was finally in the hands of the Finnish volunteers. During the following night the *Westland*, *Germania* and *Nordland* grenadiers, with all of the divisional service units, crossed the only bridge over the Manytsh River, continuing on towards Salsk. Infantryment, gunners, motorcyclists, anti-tank gunners, engineers, all were on the march towards Rostov. Acting as rear guard, the two battalions under Lohmann and Krügel of *Nordland* had taken up defensive positions in order to enable their comrades of Collani's battalion, sill stuck in Jekaterinovka, to withdraw.

Bibliography

Massimiliano Afiero, "*The SS-Division Wiking in The Caucasus 1942-1943*", MMP Books
Massimiliano Afiero, "*La SS-Division Wiking nel Caucaso 1942-1943*", Associazione Culturale Ritterkreuz
J. Mabire, "*La division Wiking dans l'enfer blanc: 1941/43*", Fayard 1980
Charles Trang, "*Division Wiking, volume 2: Mai 1942-Avril 1943*", Editions Heimdal

The Panzerschreck
by Massimiliano Afiero

A German soldier with a *Panzerschreck*.

American soldiers training with *Bazooka*.

Like the *Panzerfaust*, the *Panzerschreck* was a weapon widely used by the Germans during the last part of the Second World War, and which had high destructive power and was simple to use as well as to produce. Produced in more than 260,000 examples in the space of a year, between August of 1943 and July of 1944, judged to be sufficient for current wartime needs, in a certain sense it represented the evolution of the *Panzerfaust* thanks to the introduction of some features such as the pistol grip, the trigger, the shield and the ability to use the weapon for more than one time, which improved the design around which the "armored fist" was born.

A copy of the bazooka

During the Second World War, one of the characteristics that marked most of the German scientists, for good or for bad, was undoubtedly their ability to theorize and then to make their ground-breaking ideas a reality. There was, however, one case, and that is that of the *Panzerschreck*, in which German ingenuity was inspired by the Americans, who in 1942 had realized the potential of a single shot, lightweight, easily transportable weapon which had nothing in common with traditional antitank rifles and guns: it was the *Bazooka M1A1*. The Germans encountered the bazooka during the fighting in North Africa, learned about the good qualities that the weapon showed against their tanks and began to show a great interest in this American design. It was not until February 1943, in Tunisia, that the Germans were able to capture several examples and their ammunition, which were immediately sent to Germany to be analyzed. Studies that followed highlighted the good technical and design characteristics of the *bazooka*, but at the same time revealed its limits with respect to penetrating capability. The weapon, in fact, under favorable firing conditions, was able to penetrate a maximum thickness of 80mm of armor, which was not enough to cope with Soviet tanks that the Germans had to face with increasing frequency on the Eastern Front.

Hungary, March 1945: a German soldier with a *Panzerschreck* in an ambush position.

A *Volksturm* militia unit equipeed with *Panzerfaust* and *Panzerschreck*, November 1944.

Nevertheless, the Germans understood the basic idea that the *bazooka* was worthwhile and saw in it the ability to make modifications and improvements which could increase its performance. This perception was correct and the first prototypes of what would become the *Panzerschreck*, at the time called the *Ofenrohr* (literally, "stove pipe"), showed an improvement in performance, but at the expense of range, which the Germans were unable to increase above 100/150 meters. The increase in penetration was made possible thanks to a shaped charge projectile designated the *RpzB Gr 4322, Raketen Panzerbüchse Granate 4322*, which was the evolution of an 8.8 cm round already used by the Germans for the *Raketenwerfer 43*. The early examples of the *Raketen Panzerbüchse 43*, the name initially assigned to the *Panzerschreck*, were ready for testing around the end of August 1943 and beginning in October of that year, it was possible to begin issuing it to units at the front. In terms of performance the *Raketen Panzerbüchse 43*, despite its limited range of 100/150 meters, achieved a penetration of 95mm at an impact angle of 30º, which rose to 160mm at 60º.

Detail of the pistol grip and the trigger with the *Stossgenerator* system, used to produce a small electric charge needed to set off the round's propellant, which ran along the entire length of the weapon to its end.

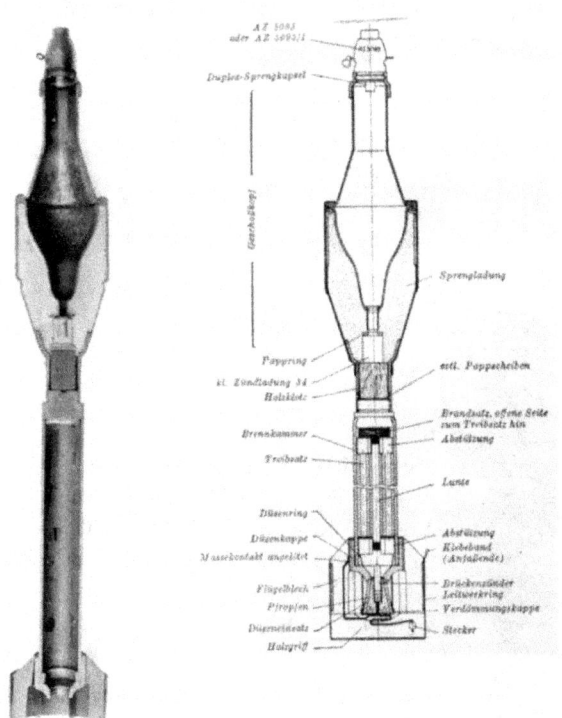

Drawing and cutaway of the *RPzB Gr. 4322* projectile used with the *Panzerschreck*.

Technical characteristics

The structural aspect of the weapon, like that of the *Panzerfaust*, consisted essentially of two main parts: the projectile and the launch tube, characterized by a small frontal shield to protect the operator, a feature which however was not present on the earliest examples. The RPzB Gr. 4322 used the same shaped charge principle as did the round used in the *Panzerfaust*. It had a propellant base (660 grams) necessary to launch it, which was detonated by a sort of internal primer, which in turn was activated by the weapon's hammer, linked to the trigger on the underside of the launch tube. This mechanism, which was mechanical, was later replaced by an electrical firing system, which was safer and more reliable.

Differing however from the bazooka, which used a battery to supply the energy needed to ignite the projectile's propellant, the Germans developed a sort of small generator, called the *Stossgenerator*, in which the discharge of the current was induced by a magnet struck by a small circular steel bar linked to the trigger. In fact the *Panzerschreck* was fitted with a true pistol grip and a trigger, but most of all, differing from the *Panzerfaust*, it had been designed to be reloaded and utilized more than one time.

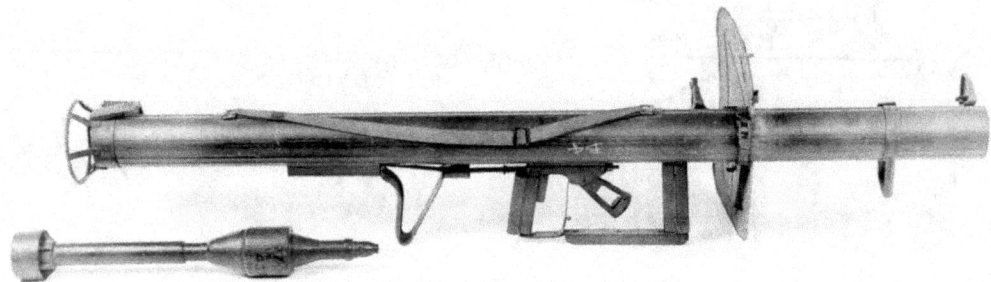

An example of the *Raketen-Panzerbuchse 54* with its projectile or rocket.

Going back to the launch tube, the early models of the *Raketen Panzerbüchse 43* lacked the frontal shield which marks the design of most of the *Panzerschreck* that were produced. It was definitively introduced in the early months of 1944 with the *Raketen Panzerbüchse 54*, because on the front lines it was realized that the safety system used until then was completely ineffective and above all unsuitable for rapid use of the weapon.

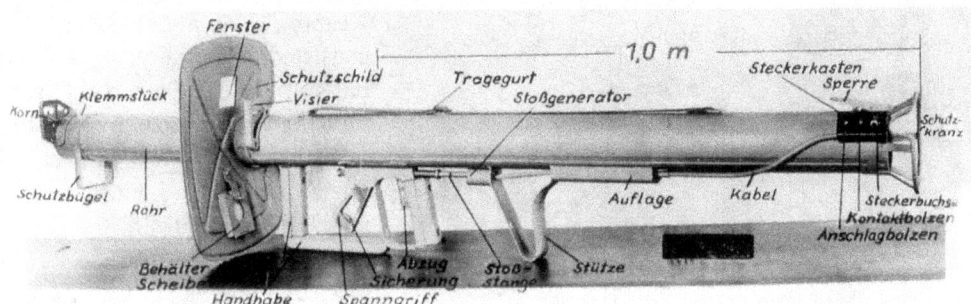

Photo of the *Raketen-Panzerbuchse 54* showing the various elements that characterized it.

A German soldier training with a *Panzerschreck*.

In particular, the procedure called for the operator, prior to firing, to put on a gas mask (without filter), gloves and special clothing to protect himself from the round's propellant, which once it exited the launch tube continued to burn for a brief period. Owing to the experience gained at the front with the early examples, it became necessary to introduce a rudimentary sight system and a support for the launch tube. In particular, this feature shaped like a "U", to be attached on the underside of the launch tube, was meant to keep the weapon away from the ground. In fact, in the event that the operator wanted to fire from a prone position, he would certainly have rested the weapon on the ground and firing it, in all likelihood, would have raised a quantity of debris which if introduced to the inside of the *Panzerschreck* would be able to cause serious problems.

December 1943, one of the earlies examples of the *Panzerschreck*, still without protective the frontal shield for the operator and he "U" support under the front of the launch tube.

German soldiers armed with *Panzerschreck*, Italy 1944.

Use of the weapon was rather simple, but compared to the *Panzerfaust* required a few additional measures and usually required the presence of two soldiers: one loader and the operator, who aimed at the target and fired. The projectile was inserted into the rear of the launch tube, after which the operator released the safety, which was on the pistol grip, thus freeing up the trigger. Once pulled, the trigger released the steel bar that was used to hit the magnet and induce the electric charge needed to fire the round's propellant. The two soldiers, however, did not act alone, but operated as part of a squad of *Panzerzerstörengruppen*, equipped with three *Panzerschreck*, in coordination with another squad of *Panzerzerstörengruppen* so as to ensure mutual coverage during the target engagement phase.

Another photo showing one of the early *Panzerschreck*.

A German soldier with a *Panzerschreck*.

During the second half of 1944, the weapon underwent several improvements to both the launch tube and the projectile. The new *Raketen Panzerbüchse 54/1* retained the same design as its predecessor, but the launch tube was shortened from the original 164 cm length to 135, with a consequent reduction in weight from 11 kg to 9.5 kg, while the old projectile was replaced by the new *RPbZ. Gr. 4492*, which was faster and able to achieve a greater range, almost two hundred meters. The new weapon was officially adopted in December 1944, but it was not until the early months of 1945 that the first deliveries to the front could be made.

Field service

During its year and a half of service, the *Panzerschreck* proved to be very effective, chiefly when used properly by *Panzerzerstörengruppen*, who were well trained and imbued with a good dose of courage, because often, in order to be sure that the round hit the target under all conditions, it was necessary to engage the target at a close-in range of 30/40 meters. Not by accident, during the final months of the war, the *Panzerschreck* began to be used in practically every encounter and became the main resource to deal with the unending stream of Soviet tanks.

Italy, December 1943: two *Fallschirmjäger* testing one of the early versions of the *Panzerschreck*, equipped with the circular front shield.

SS-Ustuf. **Frithjof-Elmo Porsch.**

This was a very dangerous job, not suitable for just anyone, which required a good amount of strong nerve and determination. That was the case, for example, of *SS-Untersturmführer* Porsch, a highly decorated twenty-year old, with a very respectable record at the front, who Otto Skorzeny gave the difficult task of preventing a breakthrough to the east of Berlin, during the last desperate attempts to defend the city in April 1945. The decision to give Porsch command of the *Dora II* antitank company, with the difficult task of facing a numerically overwhelming force, was not made by chance: Porsch, in fact, had gained notable experience on the Eastern Front as a tank killer and on more than one occasion had displayed calm and nerves of steel in carrying out risky missions against Soviet tanks.

These qualities of his turned out to be indispensable to carry out the mission entrusted to him by Skorzeny, during which he was able to destroy seventeen enemy tanks. It is enough to realize that in only three days Porsch, with very few resources when compared to those of the enemy, managed to hold off two Soviet attacks conducted, respectively, by a tank regiment and by an infantry regiment near the city of Seelow, at the gates of Berlin.

February 1945: Otto Skorzeny personally awarding the Tank Destruction Badge to his men.

A German antitank squad engaged on the Eastern front in the winter of 1944-45, equipped with a *Panzerschreck*.

This was a result which had little influence on the general conduct of the war, which was by now lost, but significant because the path chosen by the Germans with the *Panzerschreck* and *Panzerfaust* was able to provide, not only on paper, an effective solution to the needs of the antitank struggle. Time, however, was a tyrant and although the introduction of those weapons at the front was not too late, it would have been difficult for the war to have ended differently.

Courage, but training as well

The task of the antitank squads required a good degree of courage and determination along with proper training, a factor which could not be disregarded. Although use of the weapon was rather simple, if compared to other types of weapons, the Germans soon realized that focused training would preclude the danger of accidents as well as the possibility that the *Panzerschreck* as well as the *Panzerfaust* were not able to cope effectively with enemy tanks because of improper use. In fact, as easy as the weapon was to use, the particular conditions which a soldier has to face in certain battlefield situations can be such as to make him forget everything that he learned during training. The only way to avoid that eventuality is to make the soldier assimilate certain behaviors so that they become natural, instinctive and performed automatically without having to think about them.

The *Platzpatronenschießgerät*, one of the first devices made for training using parts of the Mauser K98k rifle.

To that end the Germans developed a specialized training program for the antitank units that were to be equipped with the new weapons, but not being able to use real *Panzerschreck* and *Panzerfaust*, which were sorely needed at the front, they used extremely simplified versions of those weapons created especially to train recruits. The first training weapon to be produced and distributed in the summer of 1944 was the *Platzpatronenschießgerät*, which was supposed to emulate both the *Panzerfaust 30* and the *Panzerfaust 60*. This "weapon" was nothing more than a tube fitted with the barrel and action of a Mauser 98K rifle, equipped with blank rounds smaller than the real rounds.

A *Panzerschreck* on the Eastern Front in late 1944.

The Axis Forces

A *Panzerschreck* in the Winter 1944-45.

The impressive rear jet from the *Panzerschreck* caused by the round's propellant which after firing continued to burn for a few moments.

Other devices were later developed which were more similar to a real *Panzerfaust*, from which they drew not only their form but their firing system as well, in order to make the training more realistic. In fact these devices, for all their attempts to create the same experience that the recruit would face in the field with the *Panzerfaust* and of the *Panzerschreck*, at least at first were not able to emulate certain characteristics of the real weapons, forcing German engineers to come up with solutions to avoid those shortcomings. The *Platzpatronenschießgerät* was unable, on the one hand, to reproduce the scorching gas blast that flamed out from the rear of both the *Panzerfaust* and the *Panzerschreck*, while on the other hand, having borrowed the firing mechanism of a rifle, it had a light recoil. It was thus important, even in a training environment, to recreate as much as possible the same conditions that the infantryman would surely encounter in the field. The effects of recoil and elevation, which were practically absent in the real weapons, could compromise the training in the sense that the recruits would become accustomed to taking aim and to fire taking into account these two factors, but then finding himself in a combat situation with a weapon that lacked those operational characteristics. The Germans accordingly developed two new devices for training which, by modifying the firing system of the *Panzerfaust 30* with the addition of additional features, were able to reproduce conditions very similar to those of the real weapons: these were the *Exerziergerät für Panzerfaust*, suitable for basic training on the weapon and the *Einheitsübungsschießgerät*, specifically for training on how to take aim and to fire.

Bibliography
M. Afiero, "*SS-Panzerknacker:uomini contro carri*", Soldiershop Publishing
M. Afiero, "*Panzerknacker*", Kagero Publishing

TITOLI PUBBLICATI - ALREADY PUBLISHING

www.ingramcontent.com/pod-product-compliance
Lightning Source LLC
LaVergne TN
LVHW081545070526
838199LV00057B/3788